Crystals

Crystals

The Complete Beginner's Guide to Crystals and Crystal Healing

By Lucy Gemson

Table of Contents

Introduction 9
The History of the Usage of Crystals 11
Crystal 101 – The Basics of Crystals and Crystal Healing 15
What are crystals? 15
How they work 16
How chakras tie in 17
Crystal grids 26
Setting up a basic crystal grid 28
How to Shop for Crystals 31
Determining factors in selection 33
Purchasing crystals online 35
The Preparation of Your Crystals 37
Cleansing 38
Charging and programming your crystals 42
Mental and Physical Preparations 45
Rituals and ceremonial magic 45
Basic ritual preparation 47
The Profile of 100 Popular Crystals 51
Aegirine 51
Agate 51
Amazonite 52
Amber 52
Amethyst 52
Ametrine 53
Ammolite 53
Analcime 53
Andalusite 54
Anhydrite (Angelite) 54
Apache Tear 54
Apatite 55
Apophyllite 55
Aquamarine 55
Aragonite 56
Astrophyllite 56
Aventurine 56
Azurite 57
Bloodstone 57
Bowenite 57
Carnelian 58

Catlinite 58
Cavansite 58
Celestite 59
Citrine 59
Crystal Quartz 59
Cuprite 60
Danburite 60
Desert Rose 60
Diamond 61
Dolomite 61
Eilat Stone 61
Emerald 62
Enhydro crystal 62
Epidote 62
Fluorite 63
Fossil 63
Fuchsite 63
Fulgurite 64
Galaxite 64
Galena 64
Garnet 65
Girasol 65
Glendonite 65
Goshenite 66
Gyrolite 66
Hematite 66
Howlite 67
Indicolite (Elbaite) 67
Iolite 67
Jade 68
Jasper 68
Jet 68
Kinoite 69
Kunzite 69
Kyanite 69
Labradorite 70
Lapis Lazuli 70
Leopard Skin Jasper 70
Lepidolite 71
Lodestone 71
Malachite 71
Mica 72
Moldavite 72

Moonstone 72
Morganite 73
Moss Agate 73
Nebula Stone 73
Nuummite 74
Obsidian 74
Onyx 74
Opal 75
Pearl 75
Petalite 75
Petrified Wood 76
Pyrite 76
Rhodocrosite 76
Rose Quartz 77
Ruby 77
Sapphire 77
Sardonyx 78
Septarian 78
Serpentine 78
Smithsonite 79
Snowflake Obsidian 79
Sodalite 79
Staurolite (Fairy Cross) 80
Sunstone 80
Tanzanite 80
Tiger's Eye 81
Topaz 81
Tourmaline 81
Tsavorite 82
Turquoise 82
Ulexite 82
Unakite 83
Variscite 83
Verdite 83
Wulfenite 84
Zoisite 84

Rituals and Methods Incorporating Crystals 85
General healing ritual 86
Crystal Elixirs 87

Correspondence Charts 89
Color Correspondences 90
Further Color Correspondences 91
Crystal Energies Quick Guide (Magic) 91

Crystal Energies Quick Guide (Healing) 93
For Crystal Elixirs 93
Further Information/Links 95

Introduction

Humans have been enchanted by precious and semi-precious stones since prehistoric times, whether for the purpose of adornment or for the belief in their supernatural qualities. Before the advent of scientific exploration, gems, crystals, and other forms of precious minerals had also been used for their healing properties. In jewelry and clothing, housing (building materials), medicine, and ornaments: the usage of crystals and the like were and continue to be touchstones and much more for all who are dazzled by their power and beauty.

The purpose of this book is to provide a clear resource, especially for those unfamiliar with the use of crystals. That being said, many who are more advanced in the workings of ritual or with the incorporation of crystals and gems in their healing work can benefit from this simple yet informative guide.

For the sake of simplicity, the word "crystals" will be used to encompass all levels of precious stones, although there will be times when specific names and terms will be warranted. Also, you do not have to be a Pagan or Wiccan practitioner to use this book. Many in the "New Age" movement – not to mention those working with them for healing – will find this book useful.

We will discuss the basics, involving a brief history of crystals, as well as practical examples and correspondence charts at the end – particularly handy for those who wish to incorporate crystals into their ritual work. We will explore things such as how to source your crystals, what factors to take into consideration when choosing them, and how to take care of them.

There is also a section profiling 100 crystals – including their descriptions, origins, colors, associated chakras, and their primary uses in regards to their magical and healing properties. There are also healing examples for each crystal for you to practice and even to help create your own personalized "mojo" bags or crystal grids.

However you choose to use this book, you are sure to find that your appreciation or even fascination with crystals and their uses will be enhanced, with (hopefully) a greater understanding of their evolution, practical applications, and how the earth gives us everything we need in order to live happy and healthy lives.

The History of the Usage of Crystals

Crystals have their own magical energies and have been surrounded by strange folklore, attributed with symbolic significance, and used in a variety of ways since the dawn of time. Sometimes used as currency or as gifts for kings and queens, many humans throughout the ages have gasped at the sight of their inherent beauty – especially when made into jewelry, included in clothing, crowns, or armor (to name a few), or when carved into statues or ornaments.

The word "crystal" is considered to have evolved from ancient Greece – "krystallos" meaning "ice" – as they believed that stones (especially clear quartz) were remnants of frozen water, magically staying in that form for eternity, hence their magical properties. Sailors have often taken crystal and gem amulets with them to keep them safe at sea.

The main focus in the usage of crystals has always been the idea of transformation, particularly in regards to healing. They have also been used for scrying (with magic mirrors made from obsidian or other dark, metallic stones), to increase psychic powers, or for divination – as well as the amplification of energies or the properties of other crystals (when used in conjunction with each other).

The varying beliefs associated with crystals include the idea that they can unlock hidden potential and expand our levels of consciousness – even to act as a gateway to communing with the "Divine." They provide a way to ground ourselves, which is not a stretch when we consider the fact that they come from the earth.

Even if you're a skeptic, it's important to keep in mind how the brain works – in terms of programming and understanding ourselves. When we incorporate "touchstones" for the purpose of reminding ourselves about what we hope to achieve, the very sight of a crystal can invoke the feelings and energies associated with it – therefore bringing about the goals we strive for or the energies we wish to emulate or heal ourselves with.

We've all seen images of clairvoyants and witches gazing into crystal balls in order to see into the future. We've also seen amulets and talismans carved out of precious stones, for the purpose of gaining luck or to thwart the "evil eye" (or worn for protection against negativities).

There have been many archaeological discoveries throughout the world, when ancient graves were excavated, producing jewelry and carvings adorned with crystals such as turquoise, jet, amber, quartz and other precious and semi-precious stones. (In modern times, we class crystals according to two basic categories: precious, which are diamonds, rubies, sapphires, and emeralds; and all other gemstones considered to be semi-precious.)

The items excavated were considered to have been used as talismans and amulets for religious and healing purposes. Beads and carved animals have been unearthed as symbols of totemic healing and protection, as well as adornment. Beads made from fossilized shells and sharks' teeth were found at archaeological digs in Russia and amulets and beads made from amber were discovered in Britain dating over 10,000 years ago.

There are many ancient sites with stone monoliths still intact throughout the world. Some of them were deliberately made out of certain rocks and stones, believed to possess properties that enhanced the purposes of the sites. It has been noted by scientists that the bluestone used to build Stonehenge has musical properties when played or struck. It is also believed that fragments or chips taken from the rocks have healing properties.

In the Boyne Valley in Ireland, a solar temple called "Newgrange" – older than Stonehenge and the pyramids – was built with a roof covered in white quartz, to symbolize the White Goddess for the winter solstice. Crystals have been used to decorate and empower many monuments throughout the ages. Magicians, clairvoyants, and astrologers have been enchanted by precious gems and crystals, believing them to be aligned with planetary influences, seasonal vibrations, and magical properties.

It has long been believed that each month has its own "birthstone" – and even each day and hour of the day. (Refer to the correspondence charts section at the end of this book for more information.)

Crystals have been incorporated into the breastplates worn by High Priests and Priestesses, along with warriors wearing them when they were going into battle and royalty wearing them to show their status. They were often carved into cups and other utensils, as well as ornaments to decorate the homes of the wealthy. Even prehistoric people used them as currency when bartering with each other.

Many religions have used crystals in the adornment of their iconography as well as their chalices, robes, and even their bibles and statues. Their very nature – whether highly polished or found surreptitiously when scrounging around in caves or riverbeds – brings delight and joy to those who find them. They hint at a magical world or secret energies just waiting to be discovered.

The ancient Sumerians were said to have used crystals in their magical rites. Green stones often featured in burial rites in ancient Egypt as well as in ancient Mexico and New Zealand, where they were believed to be lucky.

Many famous stories throughout history involve crystals and precious minerals. Ancient Egyptian temples (especially those that were used in worship of their Gods) were decorated with gold and lapis lazuli, which was considered to be a royal stone. It was pulverized into a paste that was used for rubbing the crown of the head for the purpose of banishing negative energies and spiritual impurities.

The headdresses worn by the Pharaohs were often decorated with malachite, believed to assist the wearer in ruling wisely. Malachite was also powdered to assist with psychic vision, wisdom, and to heal poor eyesight.

They also buried their loved ones with gemstones – including quartz – to protect them on their journey to the afterlife. Many different crystals and precious stones were found in their tombs – like tiger's eye and turquoise – fashioned into shapes, shields, and amulets such as the Eye of Horus and many scarabs. The Egyptians used a variety of different crystals for purposes such as fertility, enlightenment, and to increase their psychic powers.

The Ancient Chinese have used green jade in their statue work, amulets, and jewelry for energies such as prosperity, love, and luck. (Jade carved into the shape of a butterfly was considered to embody success in love.) They also used jade to make musical instruments and soldiers would be buried with jade armor. Dragons were often carved out of jade with quartz crystal considered to be the heart of the dragon.

In Ancient Greece, soldiers would have crushed hematite rubbed on their shoulders for invincibility before going into battle. The Greeks also valued asteria gemstones – which are crystals that reveal a shiny star shape when held in the light – for the attraction of love.

Helen of Troy was one of the most famous historical people to wear an asteria gemstone.

In Ayurvedic medicine (an Indian form of healing) the use of crystals is incorporated in their practices to aid in the balancing of spiritual and emotional ailments. In ancient India, the use of crystals was surrounded in rich folklore. It was here where the belief in chakra systems stemmed from, using crystals to align the etheric bodies as well as for the purpose of healing. Documents were found dating back to as early as 400 BC detailing astrological associations with crystals and how they could be used to counteract negative energies of certain planetary positions.

The ancient Indians believed that crystals held enormous spiritual and healing powers. They valued the ruby and regarded it as the king of precious stones. To banish the connection of old relationships they used onyx and to evoke feelings of love they used moonstone, which was considered to be sacred.

Native Americans used crystals for ceremonies, spiritual and healing purposes, and rituals. The ancient Mexicans made mirrors out of pyrite and the Mayans used obsidian for ritual as well as for practical applications. They also used obsidian for their ceremonial knives, believing that they also sharpened inner and outer vision.

They regarded turquoise as a tool for creating a bridge between heaven and earth, believing that digging at the end of a rainbow would unearth a turquoise stone. The Mayans also used quartz crystal for diagnosis and treatment of disease. Some Indian tribes believed that the souls of those who'd lived virtuous lives would be sent into crystals.

Crystal skulls have been unearthed and discovered in places such as Guatemala. What is fascinating about these skulls is how anatomically perfect they are. Some say that they are at least 20,000 years old, made from agate, quartz, and other crystals. Some are adorned with precious and semi-precious stones as well as ceramic and metallic inlays.

One of the best known is the Mitchell-Hedges skull, which is believed to have been found by Anna Mitchell-Hedges, who was the daughter of archaeologist F.A. Mitchell-Hedges, in Guatemala. The uses and purposes of these skulls is not known, although some say that they were either used in ceremonial magic or were representations of those in power, such as royalty or High Priests and High Priestesses.

It has been noted by those who have come in contact with these skulls that they have high vibrational qualities.

Even though the Catholic Church banned the use of talismans and amulets in 355 AD, certain rings and other forms of jewelry made from sapphire, pearl, and other precious and semi-precious stones were discovered.

Crystal 101 – The Basics of Crystals and Crystal Healing

What are crystals?

There are five different requirements needed for crystallization to happen. These are:
1. Ingredients
2. Temperature
3. Pressure
4. Time
5. Space

Different minerals crystallize at various levels depending on the conditions they are growing in. The proper combination of temperature and pressure is needed for this to occur, as well as the level of ingredients, heat, and the space to grow in. The movement of magma – under the crust of the earth – which produces pressure for the plates to move mountains or to push downwards creates a variety of conditions for the creation of different types of crystals.

Changes also occur when the magma heats up or cools down, as well as rocks and other material being carried away by the magma. Fractures and cavities are filled with liquid escaping from the magma, which provides the perfect ingredients for crystals to start forming. Due to the constant movement of the crust and earth underneath, the crystals can sometimes be cut off from the conditions they need, resulting in the growth being halted – only to start again with new movement.

Combined with different chemical compositions, the colorization and patterning begins to occur. These changes also create the possibilities for new crystals to emerge, which is why you might see a cluster here and there, or even several different crystals combined.

There are many other factors involved in the production of crystals, including gas, hydrothermal conditions, environmental changes, and human interference, such as mining, drilling, etc.

Sometimes fossils are thrown into the mix, producing beautiful stones and things such as opalized bones or shells. Other forms include petrified wood, "sea-glass" – which is glass tossed around in the ocean for a long time – and metallic minerals.

How they work

Crystals have been used for a variety of reasons throughout history – and not just for ornamental, cosmetic, spiritual, or healing purposes. In recent times, the ability of quartz crystals to receive, process, and transmit energy – using their vibrational frequencies – has been utilized in twentieth-century gadgets such as radios, televisions, medical equipment, sonar transmissions, liquid crystal displays in watches, computer chips, cars, and even in satellites.

From a spiritual point of view, the elements involved in the healing properties and usage of crystals can be recognized along the same lines. Healers and magical practitioners have incorporated crystals in their rituals and methods in order to receive, transmit, store, focus, balance, transform, and amplify their inherent energies.

It is considered (in the metaphysical application of crystal healing and ritual work) that crystals represent the five elements: earth, air, fire, water, and spirit. Crystals grow in the earth yet can reflect light transmitted through the air. They can project electrical pulses to create fire yet they also possess the same properties or molecular structure as water, as seen in the components of a snowflake. Crystals are therefore seen by the magical practitioner or healer as the culmination of all elements – leading to the fifth element of spirit – in the way that their energies are polarized.

Crystals can be viewed as the combination of material and spiritual energies, especially when their magical purposes are aligned with appropriate planetary correspondences and other related influences needed for particular goals and outcomes. In turn, their vibrational frequencies are considered to be the exemplification of spirit over matter, transforming their humble energies into powerful tools for healing.

In scientific terms and sacred geometry, everything in the Universe is seen in forms of waves, such as sound, light, cosmic rays, micro waves, electro-magnetic energy, etc. Scientists have discovered that physical objects can be viewed as waves or particles, where their behavior can be predicted according to the model of their wave form. It is considered by scientists and magical practitioners (or healers) that energy is the building block of all that exists in the Universe.

Whether you believe that crystals are just pretty objects created in the earth or that they are inherently magical, their energies can be felt when you attune yourself to their vibrations. For example, when you program yourself via research into a particular crystal's energies or properties, you will be able to feel the effects washing through you as you hold them or look at them. If you're feeling stressed, hold a piece of rose quartz to your heart chakra. If you're studying and need to concentrate, use clear quartz to amplify your mental capacity. The possibilities are endless!

How chakras tie in

According to ancient Indian traditions, chakras, or "energy wheels," are considered to be stations of energy throughout the body, although they are not necessarily physical. They believed to be a part of the subtle or spiritual body in relation to the physical body. Chakras are connected by channels which transmit the energy or life-force – known as "prana" – and it is generally believed that there are basically seven main chakras.

Described as a spinning wheel of light, each chakra governs a certain part of the etheric body, from the base of the spine to the crown, connecting nerve plexuses or networking branches. There are a variety of belief systems attached to the practice of chakra meditation and healing, so, in order to keep things simple, we will focus on the generally accepted and basic applications.

First, let's look at each chakra and what they represent in terms of energy, color, associated crystals, and meditations or rituals to incorporate. (A ritual for alignment of all the chakras will be featured at the end of this section.)

The Crown Chakra – (7th Chakra) located on the top of the head – is believed to represent the state of pure consciousness. It's like a gateway to the Universe, where Kundalini energy meets and unites with Shiva energy, liberating the material from the spiritual. (Note: Kundalini is considered to be like a coiled serpent in the base chakra – which represents base or sexual energy transmuted into divinity – through the journey upwards to the crown chakra.)

The crown chakra is symbolized by a lotus flower – possessing a thousand petals – sometimes represented with many colors, although this chakra is usually seen as white. Inner wisdom is associated with this chakra, along with the release of karma, physicality through meditation, the unity of mental and Universal consciousness, and the emotionality of being "at one with the Cosmos."

It is believed that the spirit travels through the crown chakra during astral projection of the spirit, although some say that the projection can occur from the solar plexus or even through the feet. (For example, traveling through the crown can mean exploration of the spiritual realms, while traveling through the feet can mean exploration of the material realms, and so on.)

As the color of this chakra is considered white, the crystals used could be clear quartz, diamond, or any white or clear stone such as moonstone. (See the correspondence charts at the end of this book if you wish to craft your own ritual.)

A Basic Crown Chakra Meditation/Ritual

You can make this ritual as basic or as complex as you like, although it is usually best to keep rituals simple as a clear understanding of your goal paves the way for greater success. If you like, you can burn a white candle anointed with sandalwood oil, with a white cloth on the altar. If using charcoal to burn homemade incense on, you could use sandalwood, frankincense, and white rose.

Either place the stone on the top of your head or hold it in your hand as you meditate on the flame. Imagine the chakra as a white disc on the top of your head, rotating clockwise as you visualize the pure energy merging with your spirit. See in your mind's eye the Universe sending white rays of light to your chakra as you continue to merge, with the idea of becoming one with the Cosmos. If you so desire, speak to your Higher Self, communing with it and asking any questions related to your Higher Purpose. When you're done (as always), record your impressions in your journal or Book of Shadows.

The Third-Eye Chakra – (6th Chakra) located on the forehead – is symbolized by a lotus flower with two petals and the colors indigo, violet, or purple. This is considered to govern intuition and psychic power, where the idea of becoming one and differentiating between light and dark and other dualities (such as yin and yang, male and female, body and soul, etc.) It's about balance between the lower and higher selves and trusting your own judgment. It's also about visions and visual consciousness, self-realization, and mastery over the self.

Some believe that sessions involving constant, light tapping on this chakra can open up the Third Eye – which is also synonymous with the pineal gland or the lateral mind – where awareness projects from as well as absorbing or receiving psychic impressions. At around eleven years of age, children move from being self-focused to being socially aware, with the Third Eye opening up to reveal a world beyond the scope of their own comfort zone. Intuition also kicks in – especially with the onset of puberty – where Kundalini can take center stage, with all the hormones running amok!

Stones related to the Third-Eye chakra include amethyst, lapis lazuli, purple fluorite, or other stones with indigo or purple hues.

A Basic Third-Eye Chakra Meditation/Ritual

Anoint a purple or indigo candle with lemongrass oil. Use the same colors for your altar cloth (if desired) and burn a homemade incense such as star anise, wormwood, and yarrow. Either lie down with the crystal on your Third Eye or meditate with it in your hand as you visualize your Third-Eye chakra spinning clockwise. Imagine things such as keys opening locks or a door in your mind opening wide. What is revealed? Focus on increasing your awareness and wisdom.

The Throat Chakra – (5th Chakra) located, of course, in the throat – is represented by a white circle with a silver crescent inside it, surrounded by sixteen petals (the color of pale blue). It governs communication and vocal expression. Akin to the thyroid, it's responsible for the energies of growth, fluid speech, and maturation. It's also about physical security. (The Tibetans focus on the throat chakra to aid in lucid dreaming, which is the art of maintaining conscious awareness during dreams.)

The throat chakra also pertains to truth and honest expression. We've all used the term "choked up" when we feel emotions taking over us and the throat chakra is very sensitive to feelings related to expressing emotions. When this chakra is damaged or affected by illness, it is said that expression has been thwarted or stifled.

It goes without saying that those who are singers or public speakers have a particular need to keep the throat chakra in check – as well as the rest of us, as expression is important for everyone. Creative expression is considered the highest form of communication, along with the sharing of ideas.

Crystals associated with the throat chakra are aquamarine, sodalite, turquoise, or any stones colored in the blue spectrum.

A Basic Throat Chakra Meditation/Ritual

Anoint a blue candle with myrrh oil and use a blue altar cloth. Make an incense from herbs such as apple blossom, myrrh, and eucalyptus. Either lie down with the stone on your throat or hold it in your hand while visualizing your throat chakra spinning clockwise. Feel years' worth of stifling the truth, keeping secrets, and other suppressed emotions melting away. Focus on taming the "demons" that have kept you in a state of oppression. After your session, try talking with someone you trust to see how effective your ritual was. If you enjoy singing, see how much better you sound and how free you are to express your true feelings.

The Heart Chakra – (4th Chakra) located in the chest area, near the heart – is symbolized by a green flower with twelve petals, with a hexagram in the center. It represents the union of male and female energies. The heart chakra is also related to the immune system and is easily affected by stress. This chakra governs deep and complex emotions, feelings, compassion, love, and well-being. Its colors are green and pink.

Unconditional love for the self and others is key here, along with spiritual devotion and passion. It's no coincidence that this is the part of the body we focus on when feelings are hurt or stressful situations throw us for a loop. Sayings such as "a heavy heart" or "heartless" can be related to this chakra being affected, so meditation on healing it can go a long way to reducing emotional pain and suffering.

In order to truly feel your emotions and to instigate healing the heart chakra needs to be taken care of through meditation and creative visualization, as well as physical well-being.

Crystals associated with the heart chakra include rose quartz, jade, and pink tourmaline.

A Basic Heart Chakra Meditation/Ritual

Anoint a green or pink candle with gardenia oil. Make an incense from rose petals, apple, and peppermint. Either lie down with the stone of your choice over your heart area or sit up in front of the altar with it in your hand. Focus on the image of your heart chakra spinning clockwise and feel the energies of love, acceptance, and emotional healing emanating from it. Allow yourself to truly feel and forgive (yourself and others) without judgment. Visualize the powers of unconditional love and devotion being released.

The Solar Plexus Chakra – (3rd Chakra) located just above your navel, under the heart chakra – is symbolized by a flower with ten petals, and a downward pointing triangle inside it. The color is yellow. It represents the digestive system, the adrenals, and the metabolism. This chakra governs personal power, energy, fear, impulses, and the conversion of base emotions into complex understanding. It also governs the many issues surrounding growth and stability.

This is the center for action, where "gut feelings" arise from. It is said that the core is the most important element in terms of keeping our bodies balanced and healthy, so it's important to eat properly and maintain optimal health for this chakra to operate effectively. Scientists have recently discovered that the stomach had the remains of what is believed to be brain cells – considered to be the remnants of the brain or cortex – when primitive humans needed to rely on the fight or flight impulse in a more dangerous time.

Some believe that this explains why we say that we have gut feelings, as the leftover brain cells are still responding to problems and emotions, trying to process data or ideas in order to ensure that we are appropriately geared towards survival.

Crystals associated with the solar plexus chakra include tiger's eye, amber, and carnelian.

A Basic Solar Plexus Chakra Meditation/Ritual

Anoint a yellow candle with lemon oil and make an incense from ginger, sweet pea, and St John's wort. Either lie down with your chosen crystal on your navel or sit with it in your hand, in front of the altar. Visualize the solar plexus chakra spinning clockwise and see the power building. Imagine the chakra resembling the sun, throwing out flares of energy. Meditate on the powerful energies going from strength to strength, fortifying your resolve and building your resistance to disease and weakness.

Tell yourself that you can do anything if you put your mind to it!

The Sacral Chakra – (2nd Chakra) located in the genital area, or just below the naval – is symbolized by the white lotus flower, with a crescent moon inside it and surrounded by six orange petals. The corresponding body parts are the reproductive organs (testes or ovaries). Fertility, sexuality, relationships, addictions (sexual or otherwise), emotional needs, and creativity are represented by the sacral chakra.

This is the center for fertility, happiness, and the joyful love of life. It's where jealousy and sexual issues emanate from, so it's not difficult to understand how neglecting this chakra can lead to raging hormones or impotency. It also governs our sexual identity and the way we interact with the opposite sex or sexual partners in general. It also houses the origins from which life springs and the creative urge – which can be transmuted from profane to divine love – when Kundalini is channeled properly.

The associated color is red or orange and the crystals include those such as ruby, garnet, and sardonyx.

A Basic Sacral Chakra Meditation/Ritual

Anoint a red or orange candle with jasmine oil. Make an incense from red chili peppers, black cohosh, and fern. Place the stone on the pubic area if you're lying down or hold it in your hand as you meditate on the chakra spinning clockwise. Feel the sexual energy emanating and infusing the area with creative waves of bliss. Visualize your sexual power imbuing your essence with the capacity for sexual love, as well as fertility, in whatever form you wish it to take.

The Base or Root Chakra – (1st Chakra) located at the base of your spine (coccyx) – is symbolized by a red lotus with four petals. This is where the fight or flight impulse originates when under threat. The base/root chakra is responsible for the survival instinct as well as instinct and potential.

Kundalini also originates from this chakra, wrapped around the knots, lying dormant. It is said that the incorrect summoning of Kundalini energy can cause madness as it makes its way up through the other chakras to the crown. This could easily be related to sexual dysfunctions, where some unfortunate individuals focus on sex to the detriment of other important factors in life – or take sexuality to a dark place, such as aberrations, taboo practices, or over-amplified importance.

The color of this chakra is dark red, black, or brown and the associated crystals include apache tear, bloodstone, and onyx.

A Basic Base/Root Chakra Meditation/Ritual

Anoint a black candle with patchouli oil and make an incense from myrrh, frankincense and juniper. The placement of your crystal of choice can be difficult with this chakra, so you might want to either place it in between your legs (or in the back of your pants!) or just hold it in your hand. Meditate and visualize the base/root chakra spinning clockwise, releasing your powers of stability and self-protection.

Imagine Kundalini slithering around like a snake – staying intact, but assisting with the release of basic survival instincts and power. Understand that you will always have enough and that you can be self-reliant in any situation – along with trusting other humans. This chakra governs the connections we have with others, so we must learn to trust our instincts!

Now – for a chakra aligning meditation!

Any time we feel out of sorts, whether it be due to emotional issues, stress, illness, or other factors, it can sometimes be due to the imbalance of our chakras. Blocked energy at any, some, or all of the chakra centers can lead to disorders and feelings of being cut off from the source – whatever that source is – due to our belief systems and so on. Of course, there are many other things that we can do on a physical level, such as eating properly, meditating, and regular check-ups.

If you feel that you're in need of an alignment, follow this visualization – or even create one to suit yourself, once you get the general idea.

First, it's important to find a "sacred" space, or at least a place where you will not be interrupted by external noise, phone calls, other people in the house, and so on. In today's world with busy family lives, schedules, and deadlines you might think that this is a tall order, but planning ahead (or even asking a friend or family member if you can use their place) will ensure that you have an appropriate time and space for a successful meditation.

It's also important to try not to perform any kind of meditation in a cluttered area that is not conducive to a clear mind and a peaceful, successful session. There are many things you can do to create a sacred space, such as lighting, gentle, relaxing music, scented candles, plants, etc.

Once you have the place and the time sorted out, make sure you have whatever crystals you'd like to incorporate for each chakra. You can either place them on your body or in front of you – on a table – so that you can feel their energies as you meditate. Think about what symbols you'd like to use to represent each chakra, which will make your visualization more successful.

For example, the associated colors and gems might be enough for you to focus on, or you might want to elaborate into

23

totem animals for each chakra. Whatever makes you comfortable!

Whether you're going to position yourself in a lotus position or lie down for the session, make sure that you will be able to maintain the position without having to rearrange yourself too much, as it might be distracting for you. Even sitting in a chair will work. Again, as long as you are comfortable, it will be a success.

Then, start with focusing on your breathing. Close your eyes and start with deep breathing. Imagine that when you are breathing in you're inhaling pure light – which will flood your body and chase away any residue of stress or negativity. When you breathe out see it as a dark cloud being forced out by the light. Whatever variation you choose, make sure that you mentally program yourself to be flooding yourself with good air and pumping out the bad.

You will start noticing daily issues, things you are stressed about and many other images flooding the "screen" in your mind. This is natural. Don't dwell on them – just let them flow across the screen and flicker away. Before long, you'll get the hang of focusing on your breathing and getting yourself to a position where you can start the creative visualization without too many intruding thoughts.

If you have music playing make sure it's suitable and not too loud, as it will also intrude and disrupt your focus, especially if there's a piece where the music gets louder, etc.
As a side note: there may be memories or impressions that are worthy of noting after your session is finished. Keeping a meditation journal is just as important as a dream journal. It's amazing what a clear mind can create – or dredge up from the darkness – in order to be scrutinized when you have a spare moment.

Once you've settled yourself and feel calm enough and ready to begin, start tensing and releasing your muscles – from your toes upwards. Do this calmly and at a steady pace. After your toes, repeat this with your calf muscles, thigh muscles and then your buttocks. This is where the visualizations start.

See your base or root chakra as a red or black ball or disc. Focus on it spinning clockwise – slowly at first, and gradually picking up speed. See the energy flowing out and starting to climb upwards. Think about the energies involved with this chakra – such as your connection to humanity and your place in it. Recognize the primal energies of instinct and survival. Know that you're safe and grounded as this energy (symbolized by a red or black mist) moves towards the next chakra.

The base chakra will keep spinning in place but the energy or mist will be rising as you move on, changing color with each chakra being activated. Then you will see the sacral chakra as an orange ball or disc. As with the first chakra, see it slowly spin clockwise, picking up speed. Focus on the energies of sexuality and creativity as it spins, releasing an orange mist.

This mist merges with the red or black mist, changing to orange. Tense your groin area and release. Visualize the orange mist moving up to meet the next center as the sacral chakra keeps spinning. See your solar plexus chakra at your navel. Tense and release your stomach muscles as this chakra starts slowly spinning. Visualize the energies of personal power emanate in a yellow mist, absorbing the orange mist.

Now that yellow mist starts moving upwards as the solar plexus chakra continues to spin. You see the heart chakra represented by a green (or pink) ball or disc. Tense and release your chest muscles as this chakra starts to slowly spin. Visualize the energies of unconditional love emanating out in a mist (green or pink) melding with the yellow mist. Remind yourself that you are worthy of forgiveness as the heart chakra continues to spin.

As the green (or pink) mist travels upwards, tense and release the muscles in your throat. See the blue ball or disc start to spin clockwise. Feel the energies of creative communication emanating out from the chakra as a blue mist merging with the green (or pink) mist. This chakra keeps spinning as the now blue mist continues upwards.

Tense the muscles in your forehead. See the Third Eye chakra as an indigo/purple disc starting to spin clockwise. As it emanates the energies of psychic power and hidden knowledge – now revealed – note the impressions as the blue mist is absorbed into the indigo/purple mist. The Third Eye chakra keeps spinning as you move the indigo/purple mist upwards.

Tense your scalp muscles and see the crown chakra on the top of your head. It's white and starts to spin clockwise. See it open up to the Universe in order to allow the flow of pure spiritual energy, merging with the indigo/purple mist to create a silvery white shard of light. Focus on the feeling of being at one with the Universe. Visualize the energies spiraling back down through your crown chakra and see this energy flow back down to each spinning chakra.

Feel them all spinning together – as one – totally aligned and open to all possibilities. Know that you have all the energies contained within you – like a walking rainbow of spiritual light and knowledge. Meditate on this and once you "feel" that you're done, sit up and record any impressions.

Once you get into the habit of performing this meditation once a day (if not, once a week, at least) you will find that it gets easier and easier each time. Before you know it, you'll be able to perform it quickly – anywhere – and any time you need a quick pick-me-up or recharging!

Crystal grids

Using crystals on their own for various purposes is a rewarding experience, whether for physical or spiritual fulfilment and healing. Combining their energies in conjunction with other gems and ritual processes (including corresponding deities, herbs, oils, colors, etc.) enriches the experience and fleshes out the scope of your work. Another fascinating method involves the use of crystal grids.

Sacred geometry is the study of ancient teachings that focus on the order of the Universe, according to perfect design and patterns, considered to be flowing from the Godhead or Creator. According to this belief, everything in the Universe was designed in regards to perfect symmetry and the fundamental elements of design. We see this in play when we take a microscopic look at things in nature, such as a perfect snowflake, the building blocks of vegetation and minerals, as well as the construction and workings of the human body and all animal life.

A basic understanding of physics will illustrate this point when you see the components of things such as air, metal, water, and so on. The study of sacred geometry would take a lifetime to complete and cannot be properly covered in this book; however, there are many publications and websites out there for you to explore. For the purpose of illustrating the usage of crystal grids, we will cover the basics in order for you to obtain a glimpse into sacred geometry, in terms of patterns and design.

Even complex patterns in sacred geometry are built on simple elements. Shapes such as circles, squares, and triangles manifest as three-dimensional objects, resulting in spheres, cubes, and tetrahedrons – along with other forms that make up the building blocks of the Universe and everything that exists within it. Whether animal, mineral, or vegetable, everything consists of sub-atomic energies and particles along the lines of Universal design.

Therefore, we are all connected by the Universal life force. Understanding this principle affords us the opportunity to apply it in the creation of crystal grids using patterns and designs which assist us in accessing the powers of healing, understanding, and focusing on the expansion of spiritual energy. There are many variations of patterns and designs, including different shapes such as hexagons, mandalas, and pentagons. Each have their own applications and can be diversified with every crystal and purpose.

You can also have a lot of fun designing your own in keeping with the fundamentals of sacred geometry. You might want to create a complex grid for a full life reading or alignment – complete with the inclusion of various colors and pictures. Alternatively, you might want a simple spread for focus on a particular issue at a specific time or phase in your life.

For example, the humble circle is a simple design with fundamental properties. It can be used in a grid for the purpose of alignment with the energies associated with originality, unity, completion, and new beginnings. A more complex grid might incorporate extra rings to create the pattern known as the Borromean Rings which involves group efforts and goals regarding inclusion and separate components working together as a whole. This pattern could also be used for cohesion in a family or work colleagues focusing on harmony and success.

As a side note: numerology is also a key component when considering the design of crystal grids. See the section at the end of this book, where you'll find the correspondence charts.

If you're a gardener or simply a nature lover, and want to create an alignment with the natural world, the Pentagon grid can help increase the yield of the harvest, protect plants, and ward off disease for those animals associated in the eco-systems – as well as increase your affinity with this realm.

You can set up your crystal grids inside or outside, depending on the weather. Keep in mind your intentions for each one and focus on whatever designs seem appropriate – along with the relevant crystals and other materials you wish to incorporate.

Crystal grids can utilize a variety of patterns and designs – either Sacred Geometry or ones you design for yourself – from basic or simple to complex. You might even go out on a limb and step aside from grids altogether, using pictures or photographs that resonate with the desired outcome. For example, if you want to meditate on aspects of yourself that need improving or enhancing (or even banishing), use a photo of yourself with the relevant crystals placed at certain chakras.

Keep in mind that it's more meaningful if your grids and crystals use the flow of energy appropriately. Understanding the energy flow inherent in sacred geometry is one way to keep in tune with the Universe as well as your desired outcome; however, you don't need to be an expert to set up a crystal grid. The various combinations of patterns and crystals are endless, so it's important to start with a simple design with a basic goal – then go on from there. As you continue to create and use crystal grids, you will become more adept.

Setting up a basic crystal grid

There are many grids to be found on the internet and many books devoted to them, so find a simple one to start with, like a circle or square, or even a chakra design, if you'd like to focus on alignment. When it comes to the choice of crystals, you first need to determine what the purpose of the grid will be, such as increasing your powers of concentration, attracting positive energy, building creative energy, and so on.

Once you know what the purpose will be, you'll need to select a Focus Stone, which will be used at the center of the grid, in order to attract, amplify, and focus the energies – channeling them through the grid. These energies are also modified by the color of the Focus Stone. The crystals immediately surrounding the Focus Stone are known as the Way Stones. The Focus Stone directs the energy through the Way Stones, which then modify and amplify the energy further – taking into consideration their colors and the patterns or designs used in the grid.

The final group of crystals are known as the Desire Stones, which usually lie on the outer rim of the grid (depending on what pattern or design you've chosen. You can modify their placement to create your own energy flow, etc.). The Desire Stones signify the outcome or goal intended for the crystal grid, which you will choose according to their affiliation with your desired outcome. The energy garnered from the Focus Stone and the Way Stones are channeled through to the Desire Stones, along the Path.

The Path represents the journey you wish to travel (or have traveled) in accordance with the patterns in the grid, creating a conduit for the energy coursing through all the stones on the grid. It is believed that the energies manifesting and channeled through a crystal grid build to a powerful system – aligned with Universal force or the will of the Cosmos – in order to bring about the desired outcome.

An important element to keep in mind when creating your grid is the visual element. This can be achieved by using imagery which is aligned to your purpose, such as happy or healthy activities, financial success, unconditional love, and so on. These visuals will keep your mind focused on the outcomes and goals of the crystal grids you create. You can either use a clear grid (for example, printed on a plastic sheet) placed over your image, or have the image propped up on your altar, etc.

The ritual

In order to activate the crystal grid, you'll need a wand. There are many crystal wands available for sale – some are terribly expensive and elaborate while others are reasonably priced. It's important to remember that the wand will be used with the particular purpose of drawing down the energy needed to activate the crystal grid, so keep this in mind when choosing a wand. You don't need to be using a wand covered in powerful stones – such as garnet or obsidian – if the goal of your grid is to foster gentle energies or peaceful meditation.

In general, a clear quartz crystal wand can be used for many rituals as the amplification inherent in this crystal can be applied to most, if not all purposes. A complicated or elaborate wand, covered in many different types of crystals, can confuse and even "over-charge" your crystal grid, essentially scattering the energies or even creating an overflow of energy.

You might not want to purchase a wand, which is fine, as a simple crystal can be used just like a wand. Alternatively, you might want to use a simple wood wand, although some believe that crystal is best in terms of channeling energy. If all else fails, your index finger (on the right hand) can be used as a wand – as has been done in witchcraft for thousands of years. It's simple yet powerfully effective. Whatever method or wand you choose, make sure that it is aligned with the purpose of your crystal grid.

Set up your altar or workspace in a quiet area designated for this kind of work, or create a sacred space, where you can meditate without any interruptions. You might want to take into consideration the phase of the moon, the season, time of day, etc. See the correspondence charts at the end of this book if you want to make your ritual more elaborate. For example, you might want to select certain herbs, oils, totem animals, candles, etc.

Once your grid is set up, start your meditation with a focus on stabilizing your breathing before continuing with the visualization. When you're ready, take your wand in your hand (the right hand) and visualize yourself floating in the center of the galaxy. See the stars and planets and feel the Universal energies flowing around and through your being. Then visualize yourself flying through the Universe. You see the stars and planets rushing by as you travel to the center of the universe.

As you arrive at the center, see everything spinning around you. Know that what you are feeling is the energy of pure power and light emanating from the Cosmos. Hold your right hand up and feel that energy flowing into the wand. Visualize your Focus Stone in your crystal grid. See it glowing like the sun. Focus and channel the energy flowing through you and your wand to your Focus Stone. When you feel that you've achieved this, open your eyes and look over your crystal grid, seeing or sensing the energy pulsing in the Focus Stone.

See (in your mind's eye) the energy flowing out from the Focus Stone and through the grid path to the Way Stones. See them glow and pulse with the Universal energy, then see that energy flow through to the Desire Stones. The whole crystal grid is now energized and pulsing with Universal energy, igniting and initiating your desired outcome or purpose.

Your crystal grid is like an energy center that will remain charged until you dismantle it. Every time you think of it or pass by the grid, stop and meditate on the flow of energy, feeling it penetrate your Third Eye and emanating throughout your body, bringing about the goals you created it for, guiding you along the path that will lead you to your desired destination or purpose. Every time you think of it, feel the power surging through you.

Becoming more familiarized with crystals and their energies will help you identify which stone can be used for what purpose. In terms of their roles in your crystal grid, take the following into consideration.

Crystals with energies related to seeking or divulging information are known as the Seeker. If amplification or empowerment is needed, then they are called the Enhancer. If you wish to banish negative energies then the stone can be called the Dispeller or Banisher. If you need protection or guidance, then the stone can be named the Guardian. If you need or want to attract certain energies, then the stone can be called the Attractor.

Coming up with your own names is also a fun and creative thing to do, so experiment and play around until you find names that sit right with your sensibilities. See the correspondence charts at the end of this book to familiarize yourself with the powers of color and other attributes you might deem worthy for a successful crystal grid.

How to Shop for Crystals

Like any hobby or pastime, collecting crystals and other related items is fun and rewarding. Think back to when you were a child, where you either came across or were given a treasure to add to your collection. How exciting it was to build your inventory while you learned more and more – transitioning from an armchair enthusiast to a full-grown aficionado!

Of course, these days we do a lot of our shopping online, which is fine for some purchases. Crystal shopping is a little more complex, as the important thing about your affiliation with crystals is your actual connection to the stones. Seeing them face to face and having the opportunity to feel them in your hands makes for a more successful find and ensures that you get to scrutinize them before purchase.

Due to some crystals becoming rare – whether because of over-mining or exhausted deposits – man-made crystals have become more prevalent. Crystals are also being irradiated to enhance or change their colors and some unscrupulous vendors try to pass off lesser stones as the more expensive or rare items. So, how do you ensure that you're getting a good specimen at the right price? Also, how do you know that you are identifying the right crystal and whether or not the information you find (on the internet or elsewhere) is correct?

It's important to start with reliable resources such as books written by experts in the field as well as websites that aren't just "drop-shipping" sites – where the content has been watered down and configured to coerce you into buying their products. In today's day and age, content is passed on, over and over – some of it copied and plagiarized from other sites or Wikipedia. By the time you do an innocent Google search and click on the first link, you could be reading a poor example of information, dressed up in a pretty or sleek website, designed to make you think that they're legitimate or the real deal.

Chances are, they have been (at best) put together by novices or enthusiasts such as yourself – or worse, by charlatans who just want to take your money, selling you cheaper or alternative versions of the crystals and products in their glossy pictures. By the time you pay for shipping and handling, you might be unaware that the package includes inferior or fake crystals and products. See the end of this book for information about good resources and reliable vendors and websites.

To begin with, the best way to acquire good specimens is to either dig for them yourself or go to a quality store in person. There are many places around the world where you can go to dig them up and it's a good idea to familiarize yourself with geology and local groups who might provide tours or access to quarries, mines, etc.

If you're not one who enjoys getting dirty or digging in the dirt, a visit to a metaphysical store or other store where crystals and gems are sold might be the ticket. It's important to make sure that the store is reputable and not selling fake or man-made crystals. Having said that, it's perfectly reasonable to buy man-made stones where the more expensive or rare ones are just not available; however, the fact remains that the pure energies housed within the real crystals cannot be substituted. Also, if the crystals come from mines or quarries where human or animal lives have been adversely affected, you could say that those negative energies have transported themselves along with the crystals.

The issue with the above statement is that it's not easy to ensure that the crystals you come across were taken from reputable or earth-friendly places of origin that also take fair trade into consideration. A novel idea involves recycled gemstones. Several companies offer these, so do some research to find out if you can get your crystals (or at least some of them) from these stores.

The bottom line with crystals is that they have been mined and extracted from the earth since the dawn of time. They are mostly non-renewable resources and their supply is finite. It's heartening to note that regulations and guiding frameworks have been developed to ensure responsible extraction and fair, ethical trade in many places around the globe. We've been made aware of the ecological impact of unethical mining through stories circulating about issues such as the "blood diamonds" in Sierra Leone and the military-supported sales of rubies in Burma.

The two main kinds of gem mining operations are large industrial mines and small-scale digging sites. Mostly rare and expensive stones come from the large operations while the other types of crystals and gems come from the smaller operations. It goes without saying that the larger the operation, the more likely it will be that they cause environmental damage and affect the lives of the local communities and ecosystems. This doesn't automatically mean that the smaller companies and operations are a safer bet as they may be poorly run by those who don't know any better or who are not as heavily regulated as their larger counterparts.

The good thing about man-made crystals is that they contain the same characteristics as the "natural" crystals – to the point that seasoned gemologists often have difficulty telling the difference. These are sometimes called "cultured" or "grown" stones, so when all else fails, opt for these rather than synthetic or glass stones where irradiation and other harmful methods may have been utilized in their production.

Determining factors in selection

The size of the crystal is one of the most important factors when it comes to making a selection, beside its quality and where it was sourced. Crystals can be bought as singular stones or clusters, in a multitude of shapes and sizes. One thing to remember is that, as a rule, the larger it is the more likely it is that you will be paying per weight, so if you're going for a rare or normally expensive crystal, you might want to choose a smaller size. Another factor is, of course, its condition. You might be dazzled by a perfect specimen, which is fine, but even the crystals that seem to be damaged or imperfect can have their own allure and endearing characteristics.

For example, if your purpose involves dealing with your own imperfections, a chipped or roughly hewn crystal might appeal to you, as it represents your current state. The fact that the inherent and intrinsic properties contained within the crystal are still powerful and very much intact illustrates that perfection is an illusion. It's what's inside that counts. Even though you might want a crystal that embodies your perfect ideal, a broken or seemingly damaged crystal might be more in tune with how you're feeling; therefore, you might have more success in aligning yourself with the healing aspects of the stone.

Don't be fooled by prices of certain crystals being inflated due to popularity either. Just because a crystal is "hot right now" doesn't mean that it is automatically justified in being sold at ridiculous prices. Shop around and compare prices – like you would for anything else. If the supplies of certain crystals are abundant, you shouldn't have to pay through the nose, unless you're looking at precious, high-end specimens.

Color is an important factor, which drives the cost of most, if not all crystals and gems. From a market standpoint, darkness and clarity are the most sought-after qualities. The more dull or faded the crystal is, the more likely it is that it will be cheaper. It all depends on what you're looking for and what feels right for you.

It makes perfect sense that, since you will be looking for quality and affordable crystals, you need to ensure that your choices are guided by how you feel about their ability to provide you with what you need in any given ritual purpose. Buying crystals in person makes this easy, as holding them in your hands and inspecting them close up gives you the opportunity to make the right decisions – along with the financial imperatives motivating your purchase. Buy the ones that appeal to both your sense of beauty and worth – along with the right price tag.

Another important thing to remember is that not all crystals are properly named. See the resources at the end of this book to get the link for "Mindat" – which will tell you the appropriate names for crystals, as a lot of stones are improperly labeled or misnamed. Take into consideration the fact that a lot of crystals have trademarked names – such as "Boji stones" – which are a combination of marcasite and pyrite. If you're not bothered by this, then go ahead, but remember that you will be essentially paying for the name, rather than the crystal.

Make sure that you do your research, especially in terms of how the crystal was treated before being presented for sale. Was it heat-treated, irradiated, coated? This all sounds like a lot of work, but if you're serious about selecting the right crystals for your rituals, you'll have greater success and satisfaction knowing that you made an informed choice, rather than just grabbing something because it was cheap or pretty.

The most important and fun factor in choosing your crystals is letting them choose you! When you pick them up and turn them around in your hands, can you feel a "charge" or the energy coming off the crystal? Some say that they can feel it as soon as they pick a crystal up. It might "speak" to your mind or become warm – or even "buzz" with a positive vibration.

Pay attention to any impressions that bubble up in your mind, such as any sensations, visualizations, tingling, or emotions triggered by holding them in your hand. Of course, we are usually visual animals when it comes to selecting anything we are interested in, but a beautiful stone might leave us cold when touching it, while a seemingly "ugly" stone might speak volumes.

Note things such as areas in your body that feel alive or that pulse with energy once you have the crystal in your hand. You might feel one of your chakras opening up in response to the crystal or a small voice prompting you to buy it. As long as you are drawn to the stone and feel right about purchasing it, you will usually make the right choice.

Also, note how it makes you feel without reading the descriptions. It could be that the seller has their own ideas about what the crystal should be used for. For example, you might see a crystal that continues to pique your interest, but you turn away because the description says it's for childbirth or menstrual cramps. You might find that the energy of the crystal is speaking to your Third Eye chakra, making you feel as though your psychic abilities are lighting up just looking at it.

When you hold it in your hand and feel that your initial impulses were correct – buy it. It was meant for you and for that particular purpose no matter what the description or even folklore says the crystal is supposed to be for. Your own intuition trumps external opinions every time.

Purchasing crystals online

As noted earlier, if you must buy your crystals online, consider the source. Are they a reputable company? Take the time to read the testimonials and reviews. You can still use your intuition – as long as the pictures they display on their website are true and accurate. Does the website offer a good policy in terms of returning the crystals if you discover that they were not what you expected or if they were misrepresented? Remember the rule of once bitten, twice shy.

The Preparation of Your Crystals

Taking care of your crystals is a way to keep their energies pure and to create a bond with them. Notwithstanding the fact that crystals are permanent reminders of resilience, beauty, and strength from the earth, housing and cleansing them properly will keep them in peak condition. It's important to remember their associated energies and elements when considering a method for cleansing them. For example, crystals with purposes aligned with the intellect, meditation, and the creation of ideas could be considered as belonging to the element of air. Therefore, a method of cleansing them would be using air — like placing them out on a windy day or using a smudge ritual.

We will discuss the different methods of cleansing your crystals according to the elements further on, but to start with, here's a basic ritual to create your own holy water, that can be used when needed.

Make your own holy water:

This ritual should be done on the night of a full moon. You will need the following:

- White altar cloth
- White or clear glass bowl
- Distilled water
- Small mirror
- White candle
- Clear quartz crystal or wand
- Clean jar or bottle

You can make this ritual as simple or as complex as you like, but keeping it simple will make the ritual go more smoothly. The idea is to capture the essence of the moon and instill your water with its power for future use.

First, it's ideal to have a ritual bath or shower beforehand, using appropriate herbs and oils. As you bathe/shower, meditate as you prepare on the purpose of the ritual. Maybe even a chakra aligning meditation would be beneficial, in order to get yourself in the mood. See the correspondence charts at the end of this book for information about what colors, herbs, etc. you should choose.

After bathing, anoint yourself at the chakra points with sandalwood oil. When you're ready, take your items out to a quiet setting in your backyard or patio and set up your altar. Using the white altar cloth, spread it out over your table or space and set the candle in the center. Place the other items on your altar, with the bowl in front of the mirror. Cast the circle and call the quarters.

(You might want to choose a deity to work with.)

Once you've done that, prepare to say the following invocation:

(Or you can write your own.)

"Hail to Diana – Queen of the Night,
Hail to the Watchtowers who witness this rite.
Hail to the Moon and the powers of old,
Bring light to the water in this bowl.

I ask that you pour your wisdom and love,
Channel the Cosmos – down from above.
Infuse this water with your pure energy,
Please make it Holy – So mote it be!"

Hold the mirror at an angle so that it reflects the light of the moon into the bowl. Meditate on the water being infused with holy light from above. See in your mind's eye the light pouring from the Universe through the moon and bouncing from the mirror into the bowl. See the water glowing and surging with powerful energy as you focus the reflected light. Continue this meditation until you're satisfied that the water has become infused.

Once you're done, pour the water into the jar or bottle and put the lid on. Finish the ritual by giving thanks to the deity, the moon, and the watchtowers. Close the circle and clean up, placing your bottle or jar somewhere safe for future use.

Of course, you can modify this ritual to suit yourself.

Cleansing

The thing to remember about crystals is that they are alive. They are brought out of the earth and have gone through a lot of digging and handling on their journey to us, so therefore they have been exposed to many elements and various levels of treatment. It makes sense to clean, clear, and charge them once they've made their way to their final destination. Who knows what kinds of vibrations have passed through them or what kind of energies they have absorbed?

Even before they were mined or extracted from the earth, they were inundated with the energy fields present within the earth including magnetic energies, pulses, and even animals or insects passing over them. They might also have been in a place where lightning has struck, sending powerful surges of energy through the earth and rocks. When they started to form, they were a part of a lava flow, grown from heat and powerful, surging energies – and that's just the beginning!

Scientists have discovered particles called "quarks", which are elementary particles of matter found all throughout the Universe. They cannot be seen with the naked eye but can be followed as they move through all matter – even concrete and iron. It is said that quarks bring energy from the planets and other elements in the Universe, which would explain why we are affected by certain astrological events throughout the year.

All the planets and star systems in the Universe affect the energy levels of every living thing in our world, including the crystals and the earth they are nestled and growing in. Once those crystals have been unearthed, they are cut off from their energy source and are "seeking" energy from their environment. If you think of your crystals as living entities, it makes sense to ensure that they are properly taken care of and nurtured in order to maintain their power and purity.

It also makes sense to cleanse and recharge your crystals to ensure that any negativity or exposure to other elements – even the energies you absorb during the day – are expelled in order for them to perform as nature intended.

Before you decide to throw all your crystals together on a plate or table, in order to be cleansed in sunlight or soaked in water, be sure to research each crystal and make sure they can handle that kind of exposure. Some crystals fall apart in water and some fade in the sun, so it's important to "group" your crystals for certain cleansing methods before you start, to make sure that you use the right method.

Any rough stones or crystals you have dug from the earth will need a good cleaning to get the clumps of dirt off them. Once you've done so, it's still important to go on and cleanse them just like the more polished stones you already have in your possession in order to optimize their preparation for ritual use.

Using the sun and the moon (or other planets) for cleansing

This is best done outside, or at least in front of a window, where the planet's energies can get to them. This is a more passive way of cleansing them and is appropriate for the ones you feel might not hold up well to conventional cleaning, such as washing in water. Arrange your crystals in a single layer to make sure that they are evenly cleansed and not blocked by other crystals. This method usually takes around 24 hours to complete.

Using the earth for cleansing (Earth Element)

It makes sense (especially for the grounding and protecting types of crystals) to use the earth for cleansing (and charging) your crystals. You can either dig a hole for this purpose or simply place the crystals on a plate or cloth (natural fibers) directly onto the earth. Leave them there for approximately 24 hours before retrieving them.

Using smudging or incense for cleansing (Air Element)

Whether or not you are incorporating a ritual in your cleansing, smudging your crystals is just like smudging a house. The smoke from the burning herbs (preferably white sage for its high, vibrational qualities) purify the crystals and clear any negativities.
Do this for each crystal – at least for one to five minutes. Alternatively, place them on a wire grid or mesh over the incense or smudge stick.

Another Air Element cleansing practice involves using your own psychic powers (although some might argue that this is related to the element of Water or even Spirit). If you are confident in your skills, place the crystals on your altar or work surface and go into a trance. Light a white candle if you so desire. Again, you can make this a full-blown ritual or keep it simple. It's up to you.

Focus your energy as a clear, white light coming from your Third Eye and washing over the crystals. Visualize the negative energies burning up as black smoke, flowing from the crystals and dissipating in the air as you continue to focus on the cleansing.

Using fire for cleansing (Fire Element)

It goes without saying that you shouldn't place your crystals in direct flame as you don't want to damage them. If they have air bubbles trapped inside they could explode which could cause a lot of damage not only to the crystals, but to yourself or an unsuspecting human or animal close by! Lighting a white candle and quickly passing the crystal over the flame several times should suffice, although you should make sure that you research the crystal to make sure it does not contain any flammable components!

Another way of using fire is, of course, the sun. Refer to the example above, about cleansing your crystals with the energies of the sun and the moon.

Using water for cleansing (Water Element)

Whether or not you choose to use running water or distilled water (preferably the holy water you made), water is an excellent mode of cleansing, unless you have crystals that should not be immersed or exposed to water. There are different ways to use water for cleansing. From a light splash to total immersion for 24 hours – it all depends on the crystal. Again, make sure that you research its properties before using water.

Running water is a great way to cleanse, although you'll need to take into consideration the minerals and other harmful substances that may be in your tap water. Surprisingly, the same goes for water in nature, whether in a creek, waterfall, or the ocean. Who knows what kinds of pesticides and other harmful chemicals that unscrupulous companies pump into the water table? So make sure that you know what's going on environmentally in your area before cleansing your crystals in this manner.

Place them in a bowl or use your hands to cradle them as the water runs over them. Visualize the negative energies flowing out from your crystals and see them becoming re-invigorated with the fresh, clean water. Alternatively, sprinkle them with your holy water and meditate on the healing powers cleansing and enlivening your crystals.

Using sound for cleansing and programming your crystals

Some would say that this is the element of Spirit coming into play. Music operates on a higher vibration (especially New Age or classical music) so it makes sense to include music and sound in your treatment of your crystals. Whether you place them next to the speakers while you play gentle music or inside Tibetan singing bowls while you play them, the energies will infuse your crystals with harmony. Even placing them under a set of wind chimes or strumming a guitar nearby will flood your crystals with the power of sound. This is a vibrational form of cleansing which is very beneficial, forming a bond between you and your crystals at the same time.

Using herbs and plants for cleansing

Another form of cleansing via the Earth Element is using plants (although it depends on what element the particular plants are aligned with. See the correspondence charts at the end of this book for more information). Take a ceramic, glass, or wooden bowl and fill it with herbs or plants that have cleansing and purifying properties, such as chamomile, lavender or rosemary. Place the crystals on top or cover them with the herbs/plants. Leave them for 24 hours before removing.

Keep in mind certain resins and other material that might seep from the plants onto the crystals and make sure they will not discolor or even damage your crystals. Again, do some research to make sure that the plants you use do not contain any volatile oils, etc.

Charging and programming your crystals

To be clear, your crystals are already programmed and charged to a degree, so it's not automatically essential for you to do this. This information might go against what many practitioners believe, but it's important to note that the reason you bought or dug up your crystal was because of the inherent energies they possessed. It's perfectly reasonable to assume that your crystals require a boost now and then, and cleansing them is a surefire way of doing just that.

Also, placing them in the light of a full moon is adequate enough in terms of re-invigorating them to their initial power. Certainly, before a ritual, it's a great idea to collect all your tools required for your working and to focus your purpose on your crystals, as well as other components such as candles, herbs, etc. Your crystals need to know how they can be of assistance. You have chosen them for their particular energies so this would be a good time to "program" them for your intentions.

When you have finished planning your ritual, gather the

crystals that you'll be using and place them on your altar or on a clear surface in your sacred space. Meditate or go into a trance and envision the desired outcome or purpose of your ritual. See in your mind's eye what role your crystals will have to play in the ritual. Send this information telepathically into the crystals, so that they are programmed with their own purpose for the ritual.

Some say that in order to "bond" with your crystals, you need to make a connection with them. Like any friend you make in life, crystals respond well to being introduced to you and your life. One of the best ways to do this is to use the method mentioned above – using sound – but a simple way to accomplish this is to simply carry it around with you or place it under your pillow. The latter is a powerful way for you two to become acquainted as the crystal will have access to your deepest thoughts swimming up from your subconscious as you sleep. Of course, you don't need a whole pillowcase full of rocks as you probably won't sleep well at all, and the combined energies of the crystals seeping into your head could drive you crazy or bring confusion and nightmares!

Think of your crystals as working partners – alive and pulsing with energy just like you.

Mental and Physical Preparations

Rituals and ceremonial magic

Spiritual people are more likely to be aligned with practices involving ritual, ceremony, or prayer. Whether we realize it or not, we conduct rituals every day, all day. From getting up, eating breakfast, and showering before we leave for work, to the way we operate during the course of the day: little rituals are involved with everything we do. When we assign particular purposes and design our rituals – taking into consideration the phases of the moon and other correspondences – we are programming our subconscious to bring about desired outcomes that move us towards our goals.

Tribal people all over the globe celebrate the sun rising and setting every day, to remind themselves of their connection to their and the earth's source of power. Some of us pay homage to the world of dreams, to the Godhead or many gods and goddesses. Some of us pay homage to material things such as money and success. For the most part, we tend to assume that ritual and elaborate ceremonies are archaic things of the past. With their costumes, symbols, strange languages, and other talismans and potions, we think of ritual as best left to the hands of the church and organized religion – if not to the tribal societies still in existence.

It's not until we start practicing ourselves that we realize the power that comes with aligning our energies and actions to ritualized magic. Why not celebrate each and every milestone in our lives? Where's the harm in programming ourselves for greater success, or at least to reconnect with the earth and indeed, the Universe? Ritual and ceremony helps us to connect ourselves to the powers within and without: the relationship between body and spirit, heart and mind, and of course, to each other.

While it's easy to understand the commemoration of major milestones such as births, marriages, death, birthdays, etc., we don't tend to think of ritual as a way to understand ourselves – even the darker aspects. Life is full of many experiences – the good, the bad, and the ugly! It makes sense to honor all pathways in life – whether they make us uncomfortable or not.

It's especially important to seek guidance when we've lost our way or when darkness hits our own doorstep. It goes without saying that we should exhaust all practical and material methods to tackle any issues in our lives (after all, we live in a material world!), but when all else fails, ritual can bridge the gap.

When you look over the section where 100 crystals are profiled, you'll come to understand that there's a crystal for pretty much any circumstance life has to offer (or throw at you!). How comforting to know that you can rely on earth's bounties to assist when the chips are down – or to assist in gathering the energies needed for success, happiness, or protection, to name a few. It's also rewarding to know that you can use certain crystals to access hidden knowledge, travel among the stars, or unearth secrets deep within your own psyche.

Combined with the creation of a ritual purpose, crystals offer a way to link our own energies with the Will of the Cosmos. Aligning ourselves with the inherent powers nestled within the world of crystals, we are given the opportunity to create abundance, happiness, and reprieve from the daily grind of everyday life – including the trials and tribulations that we encounter on our journey.

There are a multitude of reasons to perform rituals and ceremonies, whether they be for the celebration of the seasons and cycles of the earth, the phases of the moon, or for our own purposes. In today's world, most of us have been cut off or distanced from the natural phases or cycles in life. At best, we have supplanted old or archaic methods of celebration with parties loaded with alcohol or other substances. We are only interested in capturing the moment on video to share on the internet – to garner likes and followers – which is really only a two-dimensional, fleeting sensation of well-being.

In our search for meaning, we have forgotten the earth and what makes our lives worth living. The loss of that connection makes it difficult to accept the truth of the world – that we are all essentially animals and that one day, we will pass on, seemingly forgotten. Once we reach that level of understanding, it's easy to become morose and to think that our lives are meaningless. Reconnecting with the earth restores that sense of meaning and ritual helps us link back in, with the help of crystals and other natural resources.

We learn that we are a part of the earth and the Universe. We are a part of the ebb and flow of the moon and the oceans; the seasons and the sacredness of life. In order to create (or re-create) a link to the earth, we can construct rituals that help garner true meaning. Rituals should include components such as a sacred space, sacred words (incantations and invocations – either found in books or written by ourselves), music, symbols and talismans, light, aromas and plants (incense), food and drink (where applicable), an altar, and the right purpose and time.

Basic ritual preparation

It's up to you how simple or complex you want your rituals to be. Some purposes call for a full-blown, ceremonial ritual while others can be performed quickly and on the spot without much planning at all. Whatever purpose your ritual is planned for, you can follow these basic principles to suit your own needs.

Ritual cleansing: A ritual bath or shower before the ritual assists in programming your subconscious for your ritual and paves the way for a smooth meditative process – essentially focusing on the dedication to the purpose. It's also a matter of respect to enter the circle cleansed and in the right mind. When preparing yourself for your ritual, don't wear overpowering perfumes – keep it simple. Earthy or natural oils in the bathwater (or used to anoint yourself) are more appropriate. Use appropriate crystals in your bathing to incorporate their energies in preparation for the ritual.

Especially anoint your feet and crown – with patchouli oil for your feet and sandalwood for your crown. (You can, of course substitute the oils in regards to what's available – something earthy for your feet and something airy or spiritual for your crown.) It's also preferable to conduct the ritual skyclad – or in a simple robe.

The ritual: Cast your circle (clockwise for the Northern Hemisphere and counter clockwise for the Southern) and call the Quarters. As you call the Quarters, move around the circle and as you stop at each direction (starting at north and ending at north), hold out the corresponding crystal representing the element. For example: north/earth – malachite; east/air – aventurine; south/fire – tiger's eye; and west/water – jade.

Then call the deities of your choosing to witness the rite and assist you in your purpose. (If you like, you can have a corresponding amulet, symbol, etc. for the deity.) Lastly, call on your Higher Self to assist you in your Pathworking.

The following is a suggested Statement of Purpose:

"On this night, I seek (state your intention here.) I enter this circle with pure heart, mind, body, and soul. I ask for your assistance and guidance. Please bestow your wisdom and guidance upon me, so that I can be true to myself, to others, and to pay homage to the earth and all its creatures. Hail to the elements who keep the balance! Hail to (deity of choice) who will assist me in (purpose)! Hail to my Higher Self – who watches over me! So mote it be!"

Then position yourself to meditate. Focus on imagery regarding a pathway through nature, whatever suits you or feels right, such as a field or the beach, a track through a forest, etc. Take note of whatever you see, hear, feel, etc. Concentrate on just being – don't think too much or ask too many questions. Don't disregard anything you see or hear as it was meant for you, at this point in time. What memories are being evoked – if any?

Whatever spirit, crystal, or creature reveals itself to you, commune with it. Observe it, what it's doing, if it's saying anything to you or gesturing in a particular manner.

Take mental notes (or write them down if you feel so inclined). Meditate on how the event relates to you. Thank them for their presence and ask that they guide you in your life and dreams. After the session is over, thank the deities, your Higher Self, the Quarters, and then close the circle. Pour the leftover incense, water, etc. on the ground outside as a libation, thanking the elements for their assistance.

Remember to dedicate yourself to honoring your life path – as well as the crystals you chose for the ritual. Draw pictures of them, hang pictures up, and collect associated paraphernalia. Look for talismans when out and about that match the energies of your crystals. Feel their presence in your life and note any lessons they teach you. Keep a special journal just for your crystals and record any dream messages, rituals, observations, etc.

You can adjust the ritual to suit further communication with them or other crystals that you'd like to connect with, depending on the energies you'd wish to emulate, etc. Refer to the correspondence charts at the end of this book for further information about inclusions.

A great way to use crystals on the go is to prepare a mojo bag.

In order to manifest any of the energies you wish to emulate, choose three to five herbs/plants for the particular crystal and carry in a mojo bag of the related color. Prepare a ritual taking into consideration the energy of the crystal, set up your altar accordingly, and if you want to consecrate your mojo bag to a particular deity, research what deity best suits your purpose and crystal.

The Profile of 100 Popular Crystals

Aegirine
Description: Mineral silica

Origin: All around the world

Color: Black, dark green

Chakra: Base/root

Primary uses: Protects against psychic attacks, communication with the Higher Self

Remedy: Boosts the immune system, sexual power (Kundalini energy)

Agate
Description: A form of silica in various colors, with a variety of layers and patterns

Origin: Various rocks including volcanic

Color: Many

Chakra: All – particularly the solar plexus.

Primary uses: Strength and protection

Remedy: Worn or carried to attract love and alleviate stress

Amazonite
Description: Mineral

Origin: Russia, America, Brazil

Color: Green

Chakra: Throat and heart

Primary uses: Financial success and luck, communication

Remedy: Builds self-esteem, heals the heart

Amber
Description: Fossilized tree resin

Origin: Europe, America, Africa

Color: Gold, yellow (honey-colored)

Chakra: Solar plexus

Primary uses: Purification, balancing, healing

Remedy: Cleanses impurities and clears negativities

Amethyst
Description: Quartz variety

Origin: Brazil, South Korea, Austria, Russia, India, Africa, America

Color: Violet, purple and clear

Chakra: Third Eye

Primary uses: Psychic powers, dream incubation, love

Remedy: Sobriety, general healing, and instills peace

Ametrine
Description: Quartz – amethyst and citrine together

Origin: Bolivia

Color: Clear (with pink/yellow or purple/gold shades)

Chakra: Crown

Primary uses: Psychic abilities, clears the aura

Remedy: Dispels negative energy, meditation

Ammolite
Description: Opalized shells

Origin: America, Canada

Color: Many (blue, green, brown, red)

Chakra: Base/root or sacral (some say all chakras)

Primary uses: Luck, miracles, prosperity

Remedy: Increases stamina, meditation

Analcime
Description: Alkaline mineral

Origin: America, Italy, New Zealand

Color: Many

Chakra: All

Primary uses: Harmonizing, transformation

Remedy: Stabilizing energies, mental clarity, balancing diabetes

Andalusite

Description: Aluminium silica

Origin: America, Kazakhstan, South Africa

Color: Green, red

Chakra: Heart, Third Eye (some say all chakras)

Primary uses: Divination, scrying, psychic powers

Remedy: AIDS, enhances memory

Anhydrite (Angelite)

Description: Mineral (don't wear in water – it will turn into gypsum)

Origin: America

Color: Light blue

Chakra: Crown, throat

Primary uses: Contacting the Higher Self, forgiveness

Remedy: Relieves stress and animosity, headaches and infections

Apache Tear

Description: A form of obsidian (volcanic glass formed in obsidian lava flows)

Origin: America (Arizona)

Color: Black

Chakra: Base/root

Primary uses: Protection, exorcism, banishing

Remedy: Helps dealing with grief – said to absorb grief

Apatite
Description: Mineral phosphate

Origin: Many places around the world

Color: Pale green, blue (also yellow)

Chakra: All

Primary uses: Psychic powers, dreams, astral projection, creativity

Remedy: Heals fatigue, depression, illnesses of the organs

Apophyllite
Description: Mineral silica

Origin: Africa, Ireland, Italy, Mexico

Color: Glassy white/gray

Chakra: Crown, Third Eye

Primary uses: Higher Self, astral projection, high vibrations, spirituality

Remedy: Meditation, respiratory issues, and skin conditions

Aquamarine
Description: Also known as "sea glass," mineral

Origin: Africa, America, Brazil, Madagascar, Sri Lanka

Color: Aqua, pale blue

Chakra: Throat

Primary uses: Psychic power, communication, sea magic

Remedy: Lifts dark moods, happiness, heals aches and pains

Aragonite

Description: Mineral

Origin: All over the world

Color: Orange, yellow

Chakra: Solar plexus, sacral

Primary uses: Magic charms, wishes

Remedy: Increases energy and stamina, releases anger

Astrophyllite

Description: Mineral silica

Origin: Many places throughout the world

Color: White or yellow (with brown stars)

Chakra: Crown or all chakras

Primary uses: Astral projection, spirituality, protection, faithfulness

Remedy: Releases bad habits and negativities, seizures, anxiety

Aventurine

Description: Quartz infused with shimmering minerals

Origin: India

Color: Green

Chakra: Heart or base/root

Primary uses: Money, luck, business success

Remedy: Healing negativity, heartache

Azurite
Description: Mineral

Origin: America, France, Namibia

Color: Blue

Chakra: Third Eye, throat

Primary uses: Psychic powers (stone of heaven), prophecy and divination

Remedy: Meditation, clear thinking, joint pain

Bloodstone
Description: Variety of jasper, mineral

Origin: India, America, Armenia, Australia, Brazil, Bulgaria

Color: Green with red flecks

Chakra: Heart, base/root

Primary uses: Strength, power, overcoming enemies, divination

Remedy: Healing wounds, maintaining youth

Bowenite
Description: Mineral

Origin: America, Afghanistan, China, New Zealand, South Africa

Color: Yellow, green

Chakra: Solar plexus, heart

Primary uses: Dream analysis, protection, faithfulness

Remedy: Heals diseases in the head (including the scalp)

Carnelian
Description: Silica mineral colored by iron oxide

Origin: Brazil, Germany, India, Siberia

Color: Orange, red

Chakra: Base/root or sacral

Primary uses: Courage, communication

Remedy: Eliminates depression, strength, sexuality

Catlinite
Description: Mudstone

Origin: America

Color: Red-brown

Chakra: Base, sacral

Primary uses: Protection, communication with ancestors, ceremonies

Remedy: Sexual dysfunctions, fertility

Cavansite
Description: Mineral

Origin: America, India

Color: Blue

Chakra: Throat, Third Eye

Primary uses: Psychic awareness, intuition, channeling

Remedy: Dispels negative thoughts, sore throats, infections

Celestite
Description: Mineral

Origin: All around the world

Color: Silvery white

Chakra: Crown

Primary uses: Compassion, Higher Self, angelic realms, astral projection, communication

Remedy: Healing headaches and relieving stress, meditation

Citrine
Description: A variety of quartz (rare)

Origin: Brazil

Color: Pale yellow to brown

Chakra: Solar plexus

Primary uses: Chases away negativities and nightmares

Remedy: Peaceful sleep, anti-stress

Crystal Quartz
Description: Clear quartz

Origin: America, Brazil

Color: Clear

Chakra: Crown

Primary uses: Amplification, directing energy, protection

Remedy: Power and strength, clear thinking, focusing energies

Cuprite
Description: Mineral

Origin: All over the world

Color: Brown

Chakra: Base/root, sacral (balances all chakras)

Primary uses: Kundalini (masculine) energy, passion, past life recall

Remedy: Sexual dysfunctions, restores energy, willpower

Danburite
Description: Mineral silica

Origin: America

Color: White, gray, colorless

Chakra: Crown (also enhances the powers of the other chakras)

Primary uses: Contact with spirit beings and Higher Self, amplification

Remedy: Unblocking, healing on all levels

Desert Rose
Description: Gypsum (a form of selenite)

Origin: All over the world

Color: White, sandy-colored, beige

Chakra: Crown

Primary uses: De-programming, affirmations

Remedy: Healing skeletal system, smooths worry and stress, infections

Diamond
Description: A stable form of carbon

Origin: Botswana, Russia

Color: Clear

Chakra: Crown

Primary uses: Spirituality, protection, luck

Remedy: Strength, resilience, sexual healing

Dolomite
Description: Type of limestone

Origin: All over the world

Color: Pink (and other pale colors)

Chakra: Heart

Primary uses: Manifestations, originality, creativity

Remedy: Anxiety and depression, female problems, insomnia

Eilat Stone
Description: Combination of copper minerals

Origin: Israel

Color: Blue, green

Chakra: Throat

Primary uses: Aligns the chakras, creativity, expression

Remedy: Whole body

Emerald
Description: Mineral gemstone

Origin: Austria, Columbia, Egypt, India, Zambia, and many other areas

Color: Green

Chakra: Heart

Primary uses: Love, psychic powers, exorcism

Remedy: Memory and mental powers

Enhydro crystal
Description: Crystal with water/air bubbles

Origin: America

Color: Clear

Chakra: Crown (some say clears all chakras)

Primary uses: Manifesting creativity, relationships, strength

Remedy: Anxiety and stress issues

Epidote
Description: Mineral silica

Origin: Alaska, Greenland, Sweden

Color: Green, Green-Black, Yellow

Chakra: Heart

Primary uses: Enhances spiritual growth, increase s, power

Remedy: Clears repressed emotions, panic attacks, stress

Fluorite
Description: Mineral form of calcium fluoride

Origin: China, Mexico, Mongolia, Russia, South Africa

Color: Clear (sometimes colored, depending on impurities)

Chakra: Crown

Primary uses: Mental prowess, divination, astral projection

Remedy: Dispels anger, clears mental fog

Fossil
Description: Remains of plant and animal life

Origin: All over the world

Color: Varied

Chakra: Base/root

Primary uses: Past-life regression

Remedy: Resolution of emotional problems, longevity

Fuchsite
Description: Type of mica

Origin: Austria, Germany

Color: Green

Chakra: Heart

Primary uses: Happiness, increasing energy, compassion

Remedy: Positive energies, convalescence, health stone

Fulgurite
Description: Natural glass made by lightning in sand

Origin: All over the world

Color: White, beige

Chakra: Crown

Primary uses: Channeling energy, communication with Higher Self, cloud-busting

Remedy: Immune system

Galaxite
Description: Isometric mineral

Origin: America, Sweden

Color: Black with colored flecks

Chakra: All

Primary uses: Aura cleansing, transformation, universal knowledge, astral projection

Remedy: Stress, anxiety

Galena
Description: Mineral

Origin: America, Australia, England, Germany

Color: Gray

Chakra: Base/root

Primary uses: Harmony, communication, purification

Remedy: Detoxification, circulation, inflammation

Garnet
Description: Silica minerals

Origin: Australia, India

Color: Red/Crimson

Chakra: Sacral and heart

Primary uses: Protection, strength

Remedy: Sexual dysfunctions, blood disorders

Girasol
Description: Hyalite opal

Origin: Mexico

Color: Pale blue to white, milky

Chakra: Crown, Third Eye

Primary uses: Dream incubation, creative visualization, communication

Remedy: Chronic fatigue, diabetes, issues with metabolism

Glendonite
Description: Carbonate mineral

Origin: Antarctica, British Columbia, Greenland, Siberia

Color: Off-white with brown inclusions

Chakra: Crown, Third Eye

Primary uses: Destiny, education, peace, psychic power

Remedy: Skeletal system

Goshenite
Description: Clear beryl

Origin: Many places around the world

Color: Clear

Chakra: Crown

Primary uses: Creativity, truth stone, original thinking

Remedy: Self-control, muscular system, diabetes

Gyrolite
Description: Mineral silica

Origin: Many places around the world

Color: White, clear, pale green

Chakra: Crown

Primary uses: Aligns the spiritual and physical body, ancient wisdom

Remedy: Meditation, illnesses dealing with the head, balancing energies

Hematite
Description: Mineral form of iron

Origin: North America, Hungary, Poland, various European places

Color: Gray, black (metallic)

Chakra: Root

Primary uses: Grounding, divination

Remedy: Healing and clearing bad or scattered energies

Howlite
Description: Borate mineral

Origin: America, Canada

Color: White with gray veins, clear

Chakra: Crown

Primary uses: Higher Self, divinity, astral projection, spirituality

Remedy: Calming, soothing the nerves, anxiety and stress

Indicolite (Elbaite)
Description: Blue tourmaline

Origin: Many places in the world

Color: Many

Chakra: All

Primary uses: Spiritual questing, psychic awareness, inspiration, protection

Remedy: Internal organs and nervous system

Iolite
Description: Mineral silica

Origin: Europe

Color: Many

Chakra: Third Eye

Primary uses: Psychic power, spirituality, Norse magic, astral projection

Remedy: Meditation and concentration, skin eruptions, organs

Jade
Description: Ornamental and mineral rock

Origin: Canada, China, New Zealand

Color: Green

Chakra: Heart

Primary uses: Love, prosperity, psychic healing

Remedy: Longevity

Jasper
Description: Silica mineral

Origin: America, Egypt, Greece, Middle East

Color: Red (and other colors)

Chakra: Base/root

Primary uses: Beauty, protection

Remedy: Nurturing and healing nerves, muscles

Jet
Description: Old fossilized wood

Origin: England, Spain

Color: Black

Chakra: Base/root

Primary uses: Exorcism, protection

Remedy: Purification, dealing with grief

Kinoite
Description: Copper mineral silica

Origin: America

Color: Blue

Chakra: Third Eye, throat

Primary uses: Psychic powers, communication with other realms, spirituality

Remedy: Increases stamina, throat and teeth issues

Kunzite
Description: Silica mineral

Origin: Notably Sweden, America, Australia, Middle East

Color: White, gray, and some other colors

Chakra: Heart

Primary uses: Grounding, heals old wounds

Remedy: Calming and soothing, relaxation

Kyanite
Description: Mineral silica

Origin: America, France, India, South Africa

Color: Blue, Green, Gray, Black

Chakra: All

Primary uses: Dream recall, clairvoyance, astral projection

Remedy: Balances energy and removes negativity, calms anger

Labradorite
Description: Mineral

Origin: Canada and mountainous regions

Color: Iridescent blue/green, black

Chakra: Third Eye

Primary uses: Magic, dream recall, transformation, intuition, wisdom

Remedy: Eye anomalies, brain and head, meditation

Lapis Lazuli
Description: Combination of minerals

Origin: Afghanistan, Burma, Chile, Pakistan, Russia

Color: Blue, indigo

Chakra: Third Eye or throat

Primary uses: Psychic powers, divine intervention

Remedy: Communication problems, throat issues

Leopard Skin Jasper
Description: Mineral silica

Origin: Many places in the world

Color: Pink, white, gray

Chakra: Crown, base/root

Primary uses: Totem animals, shamanism, vision questing

Remedy: Detoxification

Lepidolite

Description: Mica mineral

Origin: Africa, Brazil

Color: Pink, purple, lilac

Chakra: Heart or Third Eye

Primary uses: Spirituality, psychic powers

Remedy: Calming and soothing, healing bones

Lodestone

Description: Iron oxide mineral

Origin: Central America, China

Color: Brown, black

Chakra: Base/root

Primary uses: Balances yin/yang energies, power, protection, love, magnetism

Remedy: Dispels grief and depression, stamina

Malachite

Description: Copper mineral

Origin: America, Africa, Peru, Russia

Color: Green and black

Chakra: All – particularly solar plexus and heart

Primary uses: Transformation, love, prosperity

Remedy: Balancing scattered energies

Mica
Description: Group of silica minerals

Origin: All over the world

Color: Grayish purple and other colors

Chakra: Base/root or all

Primary uses: Removes obstacles, divination

Remedy: Clears blockages

Moldavite
Description: Mineral tektite

Origin: Czechoslovakia

Color: Dark green

Chakra: Heart, crown, Third Eye

Primary uses: Universal awareness, astral projection, transformation

Remedy: Skin and hair issues

Moonstone
Description: Silica

Origin: America, Armenia, Australia, Austria and so on

Color: Mostly white, opalescent

Chakra: Crown

Primary uses: Protection, love, psychic powers, divination, intuition

Remedy: Women's health issues – especially menstrual

Morganite
Description: Beryl mineral

Origin: America, Madagascar

Color: Pink

Chakra: Heart

Primary uses: Love, angel stone, healing old emotional wounds

Remedy: Calming nerves and anxiety, high frequency healing

Moss Agate
Description: Mineral silica (weathered volcanic rocks)

Origin: America, Brazil, India

Color: White or other colors (with moss-like patterns)

Chakra: Base/root

Primary uses: Garden magic, happiness, luck, finding hidden treasure

Remedy: Grounding energies, heals skeletal system

Nebula Stone
Description: Volcanic rock

Origin: America

Color: Black with green spots

Chakra: Base/root or all

Primary uses: Removing fear, protection, power, exorcism

Remedy: Vitality and stamina, cleanses kidneys

Nuummite

Description: Mineral

Origin: Greenland

Color: Black

Chakra: Base/root

Primary uses: Protecting the home, wisdom, aura cleansing

Remedy: Anxiety, infections, blood disorders

Obsidian

Description: Volcanic glass/lava

Origin: Many places – especially where volcanic activity exists

Color: Silvery black

Chakra: Base/root or Third Eye

Primary uses: Divination, scrying, exorcism, banishing

Remedy: Removing negative energies and dealing with infection

Onyx

Description: Layered mineral – agate

Origin: Many places around the world

Color: Black, red

Chakra: Base/root

Primary uses: Protection and defense, exorcism

Remedy: Cooling passions and fevers, increases stamina

Opal
Description: Hydrated silica

Origin: Predominantly Australia, Mexico, and America

Color: White with colored, shimmering flecks

Chakra: Crown, heart

Primary uses: Psychic powers, inspiration and creativity, astral projection, spirituality

Remedy: Recognizing inner beauty, dealing with depression

Pearl
Description: Calcium carbonate

Origin: Tahiti, Fiji, and cultivated all over the world

Color: Pearlescent white

Chakra: Crown (mostly – but can be used for all)

Primary uses: Love, luck, money, business success

Remedy: Fertility, women's problems

Petalite
Description: Lithium mineral

Origin: Many places around the world

Color: Pink

Chakra: Heart, crown

Primary uses: Totem animals, spirit guides, Higher Self, anti-hex protection

Remedy: Heart issues, balancing energies and calming nerves

Petrified Wood
Description: Fossilized vegetation

Origin: All over the world

Color: Brown, black, red

Chakra: Base/root (some say sacral or all of them)

Primary uses: Past life regression, business success

Remedy: Longevity, healing skeletal system, grounding scattered energies

Pyrite
Description: Fool's gold (iron mineral)

Origin: Many places in the world

Color: Silver, gray

Chakra: Third Eye, base/root

Primary uses: Intellect, psychic power, protection, creativity

Remedy: Grounding, blood and circulatory system

Rhodocrosite
Description: Manganese mineral

Origin: America, Argentina, Peru, South Africa

Color: Pink

Chakra: Heart

Primary uses: Love, balancing energies

Remedy: Gentle healing – especially heartache and depression

Rose Quartz
Description: Mineral

Origin: America, Brazil

Color: Pink

Chakra: Heart

Primary uses: Unconditional love, love magic and spells

Remedy: Calming negative or scattered energies, heart issues

Ruby
Description: Mineral

Origin: Many places

Color: Red

Chakra: Sacral

Primary uses: Power, strength, wealth, happiness

Remedy: Menstrual problems, restores energy

Sapphire
Description: Oxide mineral

Origin: America, Australia, China, East Africa, Madagascar, Sri Lanka, Thailand

Color: Blue, yellow, and other colors

Chakra: Throat

Primary uses: Psychic power, money, protection, communication

Remedy: Meditation and calming nerves, lowering fevers and inflammation

Sardonyx
Description: Oxide mineral

Origin: Many places around the world

Color: Red

Chakra: Sacral

Primary uses: Protection, happy marriage, love, communication

Remedy: Increases self-esteem, fertility

Septarian
Description: Mixture of minerals

Origin: Many places around the world

Color: Many

Chakra: All

Primary uses: Earth magic, nurturing old wounds, acceptance

Remedy: Kidney issues and circulatory system, blood disorders

Serpentine
Description: Mineral

Origin: Many places around the world

Color: Pale green

Chakra: Heart, base/root (some say all chakras)

Primary uses: Protection, strength, psychic powers, money

Remedy: Promotes lactation, eliminates infection

Smithsonite
Description: Zinc mineral

Origin: America, Greece, Italy, Poland

Color: Pink

Chakra: All

Primary uses: Activates the chakras

Remedy: Immune system, digestive issues

Snowflake Obsidian
Description: Volcanic glass

Origin: Many places in the world

Color: Black and white

Chakra: Base/root

Primary uses: Unearthing secrets, purification

Remedy: Skin and skeletal system

Sodalite
Description: Mineral

Origin: America, Canada, Greenland

Color: Blue with white flecks

Chakra: Throat, crown

Primary uses: Wisdom, communication, literary inspiration, and creativity

Remedy: Meditation, balancing scattered energies, dispels guilt

Staurolite (Fairy Cross)
Description: Nesosilicate

Origin: America, France, Norway, Scotland, Switzerland

Color: Red/brown, black

Chakra: All

Primary uses: Represents the elements, fairy magic

Remedy: Wards off disease, sexual dysfunctions

Sunstone
Description: Mineral

Origin: America, Norway, Sweden

Color: Gold, orange

Chakra: Solar plexus

Primary uses: Success, fortune, money, luck

Remedy: Strengthens the will, dispels negativity and depression

Tanzanite
Description: Mineral

Origin: Tanzania

Color: Purple, violet, blue

Chakra: Third Eye

Primary uses: Magic, spiritual awareness, psychic powers

Remedy: Depression, blood pressure, anxiety

Tiger's Eye
Description: Mineral (including red jasper and black hematite)

Origin: Africa, Australia

Color: Gold and black

Chakra: Solar plexus

Primary uses: Money, psychic powers, warding off the evil eye, courage

Remedy: Stabilizes scattered energies, self-esteem

Topaz
Description: Mineral silica

Origin: Many places in the world

Color: Yellow

Chakra: Solar plexus

Primary uses: Love, protection, money

Remedy: Balances emotions and stress levels, heals tissue damage

Tourmaline
Description: Mineral silica

Origin: Africa, America, Australia, Brazil, and other places

Color: Many

Chakra: Heart (some say all the chakras)

Primary uses: Astral projection, compassion, channeling spirit energy

Remedy: Elevates the mood, circulation

Tsavorite
Description: Mineral

Origin: Africa, Madagascar, Pakistan

Color: Green

Chakra: Heart

Primary uses: Financial success, destiny, spirit contact, spirituality

Remedy: Heart problems, growth issues

Turquoise
Description: Mineral

Origin: America, Middle East, China, and other places

Color: Blue

Chakra: Throat

Primary uses: Friendship, luck, gambling/money, astral projection

Remedy: Grounding negative energies, balances stress levels, speeds healing

Ulexite
Description: Mineral

Origin: Canada

Color: Clear, milky

Chakra: Crown, Third Eye

Primary uses: Reflection, divination, prophecy, revealing secrets, creativity

Remedy: Eyes and brain

Unakite
Description: Granite

Origin: America, Brazil, Canada, China

Color: Pink and green

Chakra: Heart

Primary uses: Totem animals, protection

Remedy: Pregnancy, women's problems, heart

Variscite
Description: Mineral

Origin: America, Australia, Brazil, Canada, Germany, Poland, Spain

Color: Aqua green

Chakra: Heart

Primary uses: True worry stone, intuition, psychic power

Remedy: Anxiety and stress reliever

Verdite
Description: Mineral

Origin: America

Color: Green

Chakra: All

Primary uses: Kundalini energies, ancient wisdom

Remedy: Detoxification

Wulfenite
Description: Lead mineral

Origin: America, England, Mexico, Slovenia

Color: Red, orange

Chakra: Sacral

Primary uses: Ritual magic, sexuality

Remedy: Reproductive organs, muscles

Zoisite
Description: Calcium mineral

Origin: America, Africa, Austria, India, Norway, Pakistan, Switzerland

Color: Pink and green

Chakra: Heart

Primary uses: Eliminates fear, universal love

Remedy: Adrenals and circulatory system

Rituals and Methods Incorporating Crystals

There are various ways you can use crystals to help with healing or drawing their powers for magical use. You don't always have to start off with an elaborate ritual to benefit from their energies. Carrying them in your pocket or holding them against a troubled area (if healing is required) is just as effective. It is important to program or charge the crystal before doing so in order to make a connection with it and to state the purpose or desired result. This is an effective way to link in with its healing and magical powers, as well as making the purpose concrete in your own mind.

Here are several rituals you can use for basic purposes. To start with, we'll look at healing rituals and then we'll move on to other magical purposes as well as crystal elixirs. One thing to take into consideration when preparing a healing ritual is the phase of the moon. For example, if you want to diminish or dispel an infection, it might be more beneficial to conduct your ritual in the waning phases of the moon. If you want to increase stamina or build your strength, you might need to perform a ritual on the full moon, or when it waxes, which is three days prior to and including the day of the full moon.

Of course, any time is a good time for healing, but here's a quick guide to give you an idea about the moon and its phases.

The four main lunar phases are: new moon, first quarter, full moon, and third quarter, also known as last quarter. During the intervals between the main phases, the moon appears crescent-shaped or gibbous. The flow goes as follows:

New moon, waxing crescent, first quarter, waxing gibbous, full moon, waning gibbous, last quarter, waning crescent, dark moon.

The new moon is the beginning of a new cycle, with energies involving new possibilities.

This is a time when you declare your intentions for what you want to attract into your life.

The waxing moon is the continuation of the energies as they grow.

The full moon is when the power is fully amplified, where creative energies abound.

The waning moon is a period of withdrawing energies.

The dark moon is a time for reflection – and solitude. It's a powerful time for receiving revelations about the dark or hidden side of yourself and life. This is also a time to prepare for the new cycle.

General healing ritual

This should be conducted on a waxing or full moon. Choose the deity (if any) you wish to work with and the crystals you feel will provide the most pertinent healing for your particular ailments (unless you just want to make it a general healing. In that case choose clear crystal quartz or maybe howlite).

You will need:

A blue candle anointed with sandalwood oil, your crystal of choice, a blue altar cloth (or white, if you prefer), incense made from sandalwood, frankincense, and myrrh (or rosemary, salt, and white rose petals if you want to keep it simple). Lastly, you'll need a smudge stick made with white sage if you can get it. Alternatively, make your own smudge stick with rosemary.
Prepare your altar and sacred space after you've performed a ritual bathing or at least anointed your chakra points with the sandalwood oil. Once you are ready, cast the circle and call the quarters and the deity of your choice (if so inclined). Then state your purpose, which you have written beforehand. Something along the following lines:

"Hail to the watchtowers, I call on thee to guard this circle and witness this rite.

Hail to (deity – including a few short words of devotion, such as: Hail to thee Diana – Goddess of the Moon and the Hunt). I call on thee to guard this circle and witness this rite.

I ask for a powerful cleansing, to rid my body of all impurities and to flush away any negative energies that cling to my soul. I dedicate my path to clean living and spiritual clarity."

Light the candle and say aloud: "As this candle burns, so too does the muck and the mire, burning away in the smoke and the fire."

Light the smudge stick and walk around the circle clockwise. Visualize the purification taking place, permeating your aura and flushing out the negativities. Once you've made it back to the altar, place the smudge stick on a plate that you have placed there, or next to the candle.

Meditate while you hold the crystal over the smoke of the smudge stick. Imagine the crystal absorbing the cleansing properties of the smoke, then either place it in a mojo bag or put it in your pocket. You might even want to make a pendant from it by using a leather thong or ribbon. This would be a good time to incorporate chakra alignment. If not, do a simple meditation and visualize your body glowing with radiance.

After the ritual, thank the quarters and the deity (if you invited one); put the candle out so you can burn it again each night until it's gone. Do the same with the smudge stick. Close the circle and clean up, then record any impressions in your journal or Book of Shadows.

Crystal Elixirs

Creating elixirs is a fun and rewarding way of harnessing the powerful energies inherent in your crystals; however, it's important to use the right ones, as some can be harmful or can be damaged by immersing in water. Do some research to make sure that the crystals you'd like to use will not present these problems.

The same healing principles used in carrying crystals are reflected in crystal elixirs, with the exception that you will be taking their essence internally, so once again, make sure the crystals you choose will not be toxic! (See the Crystal Elixir correspondence chart in the next section for examples.)

To create your own elixir, take a clean glass jug, jar, or bowl. (Make sure they are either clear or the color most aligned with your crystal and purpose.) Make sure that you are using a cleansed and charged crystal. Place it in the vessel and fill it with distilled or filtered tap water. Cover the vessel with either a cloth or plate to keep out impurities and place it outside or in front of a window, so the light can activate the energy of the crystal.

Leave for around 12–24 hours. You might want to leave it in the moonlight depending on the elixir and purpose. When done, either seal in prepared bottles or leave in the vessel you chose to "steep" the crystal in. Depending on the crystal, you may be able to leave it in, although it's probably a good practice to take it out.

To take the elixir, you can either place a few drops on your tongue when you feel it's needed or dilute in a glass of distilled or spring water. You can also use it like perfume on your pulse points (or chakra points), pour it into a spray bottle to use in your sacred space, pour it into your bath water, or even use in cooking. It's up to you and your imagination!

Correspondence Charts

(Please note that these correspondences are suggestions. Feel free to mix it up to suit your particular needs.)

PURPOSE	DEITY	COLOR	PLANT	CRYSTAL	ELEMENT
Contacting Higher Self	Isis	White	Sandalwood	Howlite	Spirit
Personal Power	Mithras	Red (or Orange)	Dragonsblood	Carnelian	Fire
Transformation	Morrighan	Black	Yarrow	Obsidian	Earth
Love	Aphrodite	Pink	Rose	Rose Quartz	Water
Divination	Odhin	Purple	Frankincense	Hematite	Water
Exorcism	Kali	Black	Pepper	Jet	Earth
Healing	Kuan Yin	Blue	Aloe Vera	Moonstone	Water
Dreams	Morpheus	Navy Blue	Valerian	Smoky Quartz	Water
Grief	Anubis	Black	Pine	Lapis Lazuli	Earth
Mental Powers	Thoth	Orange	Celery	Amethyst	Air
Communing with Nature	Cernunnos/Green Man	Green	Fern	Moss Agate	Earth
Sexuality	Eros	Red	Hibiscus	Garnet	Fire
Justice	Maat	Red	Marigold	Agate	Fire
Depression	Baldur	Violet	Lavender	Aquamarine	Air
Meditation	Buddha	White	Bodhi	Clear Quartz	Air
Astral Travel	Arianrhod	Silver	Poplar	Fluorite	Spirit
Success	Osiris	Gold	Cinnamon	Pyrite	Fire
Protection	Bastet	White	Sandalwood	Agate	Earth
Creativity	Ptah	Green	Ginseng	Opal	Spirit
Crossroads - Decisions	Hecate	Navy Blue	Damiana	Aventurine	Earth
Psychic Power	Brigit	Purple	Mugwort	Tanzanite	Water
Fertility	Inanna	Orange	Peach	Sardonyx	Earth
Freedom	Artemis	White	Sage	Lodestone	Air
Harvesting	Ceres	Green	Oak	Septarian	Earth
Journeys	Janus	Yellow	Wormwood	Sodalite	Air
Order	Athena	White	Olive	Kyanite	Earth
Prosperity	Ganesha	Green	Tulip	Tiger Eye	Water
Luck	Kupala	Green	Bamboo	Jade	Water
Rebirth	Horus	Gold	Frankincense	Amber	Fire

Color Correspondences

Color	Power
Clear	Clarity, single-mindedness, clear conduit to external energies, connectivity, meditation, cleansing and clearing, truth
White	Full moon magic, peace, protection, purity, balance, enlightenment, the Goddess, can be used as a substitute for other colors, purification
Silver	Also for the Goddess, mental clarity, fairy magic, astral travel, dreams, warding off negativity, pure thoughts, travel to other dimensions
Gray	Shadow work, travel to the other side, vision quests, veiling and shielding, cancellation, neutrality, freezing or halting a bad situation
Light Pink	Gentle energy and healing, happiness, childhood, childish abandon, unconditional love, compassion
Pink	Love, romantic love, friendship, femininity, service, honor, affection, healing the heart and emotions
Orange	Communication, energy, intellect, stimulation, attraction, confidence, power, control, adaptability, luck, enthusiasm
Red	Strength, passion, power, strong energy, health, anger, lust, courage, sexual or mature love, fertility, willpower
Violet	Spirituality, strong or long-term friendship, relaxation, self-improvement, intuition, psychic impressions, prophetic dreams
Purple	Spiritual power, success, idealism, psychic power, ambition, independence, divination, philosophical thought, occult wisdom
Indigo	Karma, deep meditation, access to other spiritual planes, spirit communication, ancient wisdom, clairvoyance and clairaudience
Blue	Healing the physical body, guidance, influence, emotionalism, true friendship, justice, understanding, change, coolness
Light Blue	Tranquility, peace, safety, patience, gentle

	healing and protection of the physical body, faith, devotion, harmony
Dark Green	Social situations, fecundity, legal matters, deep healing, ambition, greed, jealousy, agriculture, growth
Green	Earth, plant and nature magic, financial luck, employment, prosperity, abundance, rejuvenation and regeneration
Yellow	Activity, unity, artistic creativity, compelling, concentration, intellectual growth, alertness, learning

Further Color Correspondences

Color	Power
Gold	Supremacy, Cosmic power, riches, great success, The God, physical strength, achievement, great skills, fortune
Brown	Protection, grounding, earthly, balance, material possessions, decisiveness, understanding, telepathy, location of lost objects, endurance
Black	Banishing, the unknown, secrets, strong protection, the Universe, night, dark magic, binding, unconscious, uncrossing, lifting hexes

Crystal Energies Quick Guide (Magic)

Energies	Crystals
Beauty	Amber, Coral, Jasper, Opal
Business Success	Bloodstone, Malachite, Aventurine
Courage	Tiger's Eye, Carnelian, Amethyst
Divination	Lapis Lazuli, Moonstone, Fluorite

Dreams	Azurite, Smoky Quartz, Amethyst
Astral Projection	Clear Quartz, Opal, Fluorite
Communication	Carnelian, Sardonyx, Celestite
God	Gold, Pyrite, Sunstone
Goddess	Silver, Moonstone, Diamond
Grounding	Hematite, Obsidian, Turquoise
Protection	Clear Quartz, Jet, Serpentine
Money	Amazonite, Tsarvorite, Aventurine
Happiness	Rose Quartz, Aquamarine, Moss Agate
Spiritual Healing	Agate, Sapphire, Turquoise
Love	Rose Quartz, Pink Tourmaline, Pearl
Luck	Malachite, Amber, Alexandrite
Meditation	Clear Quartz, Sodalite, Sapphire
Peace	Aquamarine, Calcite, Malachite
Psychic Powers	Amethyst, Lapis lazuli, Emerald
Purification	Amber, Galena, Jet
Sexual Power	Garnet, Carnelian, Wulfenite
Spirituality	Howlite, Lepidolite, Opal
Success	Amazonite, Gold, Topaz
Wisdom	Jade, Lapis Lazuli, Sodalite

Crystal Energies Quick Guide (Healing)

Issue	Crystal
Headaches	Anhydrite, Celestite, Bowenite
Throat	Aquamarine, Kinoite, Aquamarine
Skeletal	Glendonite, Moss Agate, Petrified Wood
Muscular	Goshenite, Jasper, Wulfenite
Women's problems	Moonstone, Pearl, Unakite
Diabetes	Analcime, Girasol, Goshenite
Depression	Apatite, Opal, Sunstone
Heart	Amazonite, Bowenite, Opal
Circulatory	Pyrite, Septarian, Zoisite
Stress/Anxiety	Celestite, Citrine, Galaxite
Infections	Anhydrite, Cavansite, Nuummite
Skin	Apophyllite, Iolite, Moldavite

For Crystal Elixirs

Crystal	Purpose
Amber	Anti-depression, protection
Amethyst	Independence, spirituality
Aquamarine	Anti-stress
Aventurine	Strength and focus
Black Tourmaline	Grounding and banishing
Bloodstone	Cleansing the blood
Carnelian	Throat issues
Citrine	Stimulation and energizing
Diamond	Divinity and pure thoughts
Emerald	Opens and heals the heart
Fluorite	Aligning the physical and spiritual bodies

Garnet	Sexual power and fertility
Jade	Peace
Lapis Lazuli	Opens the Third Eye chakra and increases psychic power
Moonstone	Feminine energy and healing female troubles
Quartz Clear	Total cleanse – body, mind, and spirit
Rose Quartz	To combat fear and promote trust
Smoky Quartz	Detoxification
Tiger's Eye	Confidence and dealing with anger

Further Information/Links

http://www.mindat.org/

Mindat.org has been running since October 2000 with the aim of building and sharing information about minerals, their properties, and where they are found.
It is now the world's largest public database of mineral information with an army of worldwide volunteers adding and verifying new information daily.

http://www.pelhamgrayson.com/

Wholesale "New Age-Metaphysical" Crystals, Minerals, Healing Stones, and Gemstone Supplier

http://geology.com/

Geology.com is one of the internet's leading websites for earth science news and information.

http://www.rockshopwholesale.com/

We import high quality mineral, gemstone, and fossil products from well-established ethical sources around the globe.

Manufactured by Amazon.ca
Bolton, ON